The story of Mill Reef

The story of
Mill Reef

JOHN OAKSEY

London
Michael Joseph

First published in Great Britain by MICHAEL JOSEPH LTD
52 Bedford Square, London WC1B 3EF
1974
ISBN 0 7181 1188 5

Set and printed in Great Britain by
Tonbridge Printers Ltd, Peach Hall Works, Tonbridge, Kent
in Baskerville eleven on thirteen point on paper supplied by
P. F. Bingham Ltd, and bound by James Burn
at Esher, Surrey

Contents

Illustrations

Prologue

On 28 August, 1972, Mr Paul Mellon announced, to a surprised but delighted racing world, that his Derby and Prix de l'Arc de Triomphe winner, Mill Reef, would stay in training as a five-year-old.

Two days later, at eight o'clock on a glorious sunny morning, Ian Balding stood half way up the seven furlong gallop at Kingsclere – a strip of springy grass forty-five yards wide and a little longer than its name suggests. The gallop runs uphill along a shoulder of Cannon Heath Down in Hampshire and from it, on a clear day, you can see across three counties. To the trainer, that morning, it seemed about as good a place to be as any in the world. His eyes were fixed, not on the view, but on two horses swinging gaily up towards him. As they passed, hooves almost silent on the velvet turf, he strained his ears to analyse the sound and rhythm of their breathing. But there was no false note, no ominous whistle to be heard and, turning away to watch the next pair up, he felt, for the first time in many anxious clouded weeks, that the sun might really have begun to shine. For one of the two horses was Mill Reef and for that brief happy moment, Ian Balding was convinced that all his various troubles were at last behind him.

Then something made him turn and look once more uphill. And as he did so, all the clouds rolled back, far darker and more threatening than before.

Three hundred yards away, the familiar small bay figure had come to a full-stop. His rider was already dismounted

9

beside him and even at that distance, their shared bewilder-
ment and pain were unmistakable.

For Mill Reef there was, after all, to be no happy ending :
not on the racecourse anyway. Indeed, as he stood forlorn
that morning with three bones broken in his near foreleg, the
future – even his survival – lay in grievous doubt.

When the news of his injury was made public, millions
of men and women who had never seen him in the flesh felt
a sense of real personal sadness. In just three years of cheerful
service, Mill Reef had given more pleasure and excitement
than most men generate in a lifetime. The debt we owe him
cannot be paid but here, with gratitude and admiration, is his
story.

Many people have helped me in writing it. I must thank
first Paul Mellon and Ian Balding, without whose kindness
and encouragement I should not have got beyond the pro-
logue. Mr Mellon's staff at Rokeby, especially his American
trainer Elliott Burch, made the transatlantic part of my
researches entirely pleasurable, while at Kingsclere Bill
Palmer, John Hallum, Bill Jennings, Tom Reilly and many
others answered my endless questions with unfailing courtesy.
Emma Balding's scrapbook was invaluable and her mother
has, not for the first time, corrected me on important points
of fact.

I wish that I had succeeded in capturing Geoff Lewis's
sense of humour as well as the film 'Something to Brighten
the Morning' does, and am very grateful to Brough Scott and
Kit Owen, that small masterpiece's producer and director,
for letting me see their work's fruit far in advance.

For many details of the operation I am indebted to Miss
Dorothy Laird of the Racing Information Bureau, while
Peter Scott-Dunn kindly checked my clinical description.

Lastly I should like to thank Mrs Megan Feacham who
long ago accepted my endless procrastination and, when my
publishers overcame it, deciphered and typed my illegible
scrawl.

JOHN OAKSEY

CHAPTER ONE

Paul Mellon

A racehorse's fate depends, often too closely for his own good, on the character, preferences and background of the human beings into whose hands he happens to fall. For horses as for men the unfair chance of birth can be decisive and in that sense Mill Reef was certainly born with a silver manger in his box.

But quite apart from the fact that he was bred by a very rich man there were many other links in the chain of circumstance which led to his career. Without some of them he might never have been born at all – without others he would certainly never have arrived at Kingsclere. And of all those links none was more important than his owner's life-long love affair with England and with the arts and letters and variety of England's countryside and sport.

Paul Mellon's mother was English and, for the first seven years of his life, 1907 to 1914, the family spent almost every summer in England. Years later, at the opening of an exhibition in Virginia, Mr Mellon recalled those years. 'From them,' he said, 'I remember huge dark trees in rolling parks, herds of small friendly deer, flotillas of white swans on the Thames, dappled tan cows in soft green fields, the grey mass of Windsor Castle towering in the distance against a background of golden summer clouds; soldiers in scarlet and bright metal, drums and bugles, troops of grey horses; laughing ladies in white with gay parasols, men in impeccable white flannels and striped blazers, and always behind them and behind everything the grass was green, green, green.'

Well, the cynic will say, he did not live much in Manchester or Birmingham; and no one, least of all Mr Mellon, denies that this was a somewhat romanticised picture of England, even in those last sunlit days of peace. But it was nevertheless the picture one little boy carried back with him to America, and his next four years served only to make it seem more vivid and desirable. For they were spent mostly in Pittsburgh – a gloomy city where steel was king and where, each night in the big late-Victorian house, 'every aperture was covered with cheese-cloth and all the furniture draped in sheets to keep out the constantly settling soot'.

On the walls of that house, however, there hung reminders of a brighter, greener world. The first painting Paul Mellon can remember was a Romney of a little girl, Miss Willoughby. His father's collection already included others by Gainsborough, Reynolds, Lawrence, Hoppner and Raeburn. Their elegant subjects smiled down with what seemed a warm and friendly glow and, to the young Paul Mellon's golden memories of England, they added the seeds of an abiding passion for English art. Four years at Yale, which then boasted perhaps the finest teachers of English Literature in the world, did nothing to suppress that passion. On the contrary, as Mr Mellon said in the speech already quoted, 'They pushed me further over the brink into a state of galloping anglophilia'.

His actual galloping had been distinctly limited until then, and it was at Cambridge, where he went in 1929, that horses began for the first time to play an important part in his life. Paul Mellon's first sporting inclinations were, in fact, aquatic – he rowed for Clare College two years running – but during the winter of 1929 an American friend, Charles 'Chunky' Hatfield, persuaded him that their education would be incomplete without experience of English fox-hunting.

In their first ventures with the Fitzwilliam they must have been a memorable sight, these two, if only because the bold

Hatfield weighed fifteen stone with a circumference nearly equal to his height, about five feet! And although Paul Mellon was – and still is – a more conventional shape, he had then 'only the vaguest idea of the form and customs of the chase'.

The weapons employed by this intrepid pair for overcoming their inexperience included Chunky's ever-present flask of brandy, known to him as 'bottled courage', and some large half-bred hunters hired from the famous Melton dealer Harry Beeby, father of George Beeby who trained Lord Bicester's magnificent squadron of chasers after the war. Two of these hunters, Guardsman and Grenadier, were the first horses Mr Mellon ever bought on his own account. And, though a far cry from Mill Reef, they made their contribution to his story by preserving their owner's neck intact throughout two hazardous, eventful seasons.

His neck was frequently imperilled however, notably by a flashy chestnut thoroughbred called Fashion, whom, according to his previous owner, 'a little child could handle'. Perhaps by 'handle' he meant 'pat' because Fashion, though elegant and kind at rest, turned out to have neither brakes nor steering when in motion. Much admired at the first meet to which Mr Mellon took him he crashed through half-a-dozen fences, caused carnage in several gateways and ended up circumnavigating a providential grass field in ever-decreasing circles.

Undaunted by this and other escapades ('Cries of "How dare you, Sir!" seemed to follow us everywhere'), Paul Mellon pursued his education in Leicestershire and, after leaving Cambridge, with the VWH Cricklade, the Heythrop, the Beaufort and the Bathurst. About this time, his mother gave him an Irish-bred hunter called Dublin who could not only 'jump the Eiffel Tower', but was fast enough to run without disgrace in point-to-points. He, more than any other horse, set the seal on his devoted owner's addiction to fox-hunting in all its forms.

That addiction has never lost its grip and, himself a master of hounds for several years in Virginia, Mr Mellon has spent many happy winter holidays since the war satisfying it in various parts of England. The day after one Gimcrack Dinner, for instance, he removed any lingering after-effects of York Racecourse's famous hospitality by diving head first into one of Yorkshire's deepest ditches. On another outing with the same pack (the Middleton) he had subsided backwards 'into a very cold stream on a very cold day' and learnt afterwards that the local farmers (who could not have been kinder at the time) now refer to him as the 'water Mellon'.

Not all lovers of hunting feel the same about racing, and Mill Reef might still never have existed if Paul Mellon had heeded his father's only known comment on the Sport of Kings: 'Any damned fool knows that one horse can run faster than another.' Those crushing and undeniably truthful words were inspired by the purchase of Mellon junior's first racehorse – a big Irish bred gelding called Drinmore Lad. And happily there turned out to be nothing either damned or foolish about his owner's choice. Drinmore Lad (whose latter day reincarnation Drinny's Double won the NH two mile Champions Chase in 1967) was soon establishing his reputation over timber in America. When brought to England he not only won, among other good races, the Valentine Chase at Aintree but also ran a memorable dead heat with Golden Miller at Gatwick, admittedly in the evening of that great horse's long career.

It was while Mr Mellon was honeymooning in England in 1935 that the late F. Ambrose Clarke, who had already won a Grand National with Kellsboro Jack, suggested that Drinmore Lad be brought to England. So Paul Mellon was taken down to Wroughton and introduced to Mrs Aubrey Hastings, on whose husband's death five years before Ivor Anthony had taken over the famous yard.

The box from which Brown Jack went out to win six years running at Royal Ascot had only just been vacated.

Peter Hastings was a schoolboy of fifteen already playing the superlative Rugby football which won him an English cap in the wartime years, and another fine footballer, Ian Balding, was not yet born. But all the same, when Drinmore Lad arrived at Wroughton a bond of trust and friendship was forged between Paul Mellon and the Hastings family. It has never been broken since and, eighteen years later it brought across the Atlantic a small bay yearling with a bright mahogany coat.

CHAPTER TWO

Rokeby

The first English flat race Paul Mellon ever saw was the 1929 Cambridgeshire and, in retrospect, there could have been no more appropriate introduction for a future breeder of good horses. The winner that year was Double Life, dam of Precipitation and Persian Gulf, grandam of Meld and great grandam of Charlottown; one of the most successful brood mares, in fact, of the century.

At the time, however, not being blessed with second sight, it was the English racing scene in general – and Newmarket in particular – which seized the young undergraduate's imagination. Forty years later in his Gimcrack Speech he harked back to 'those long soft eminently green gallops stretching to the horizon in the slanting afternoon sun' and 'the late October light on the warm yellow stone of the old high stands'. Not all observers would agree with this idyllic picture of the Rowley Mile, but no one can deny the vivid contrast it provides to the uniform dirt circuits of Belmont, Aqueduct and Hialeah.

It was at Newmarket too that Mr Mellon had his first important flat-racing success in England, when Midsummer Night II splashed through hock-deep mud to win the 1960 Cambridgeshire. He had then already been buying yearlings in this country for some time and, in June 1949, when the late Lord Portal's bloodstock was sold by Tattersalls, his American trainer, Jim Ryan, came over to Newmarket on the lookout.

There was in that dispersal catalogue an unraced two-year-old filly called Red Ray, who, whatever her potential as a racehorse, had two powerful attractions to any would-be breeder. One was her sire, Hyperion, and the other her grandam, Black Ray, a marvellous matron who had nineteen foals in nineteen consecutive years, ten of whom won thirty-five races between them.

In Black Ray's huge and talented family, there were two full sisters, both by Ethnarch. One of them, Eclair, not only won seven races herself, but was the dam of Khaled (by Hyperion), who won the Coventry, Middle Park and St James's Palace Stakes and, exported to America by his owner, the Aga Khan, became one of the most successful stallions ever to stand in California. The other sister, Red Ray's dam, Infra Red, won the Princess Elizabeth Stakes at Epsom, finished fourth in Galatea II's One Thousand Guineas and produced among others the good sprinter Magic Red. Two of her daughters were Red Briar (dam of Big Berry and Pipe of Peace) and Excelsa (dam of the Goodwood and Doncaster Cup winner, Exar).

Much of this of course could not be known in 1949, but it is easy to see why the bids flew thick and fast when Red Ray entered the sale ring. The snag was that Jim Ryan and Mr Mellon had agreed a 'limit' of £10,000 – and in no time at all, that figure was passed. Happily, however, there stood at Ryan's elbow the genial and immensely knowledgeable figure of 'The Scout' – otherwise Clive Graham. As I write, Clive, who joined the *Daily Express* straight from Eton at the age of eighteen, must in terms of long service and experience be the elder statesman of the racing press room. But if that title suggests pomposity or a tendency to treat life as anything but a huge joke, forget it. Clive's philosophy has always been close to that of a cheerful schoolboy playing truant and more than forty years on racecourses around the world have signally failed to alter it.

Behind his unquenchable sense of humour moreover, there

lies a shrewd and agile brain. So now, when Jim Ryan hesitated briefly, uncertain whether to risk a bid beyond his limit, Clive supplied the necessary encouragement. And although the winnings took a long time to collect, the Scout had tipped yet another winner.

On returning to America, having bought Red Ray for twelve thousand guineas, Jim Ryan offered to keep the filly himself if Paul Mellon did not want her. And when, four years later, Red Ray died, leaving only two surviving foals, one of them a fairly undistinguished gelding called Claret, her owner may well have regretted refusing that offer. But patience is almost as vital as a long purse and an optimistic nature in the business of thoroughbred breeding and now, at last, the powerful genes in Black Ray's blood began to reappear, reinforced admittedly by some of the best stallions in the American stud book. Although Red Ray's third and last foal, Virginia Water (by the American Triple Crown winner, Count Fleet), could not herself be trained, she produced four winners. Milan Mill was not one of them but another, a fine big filly called Berkeley Springs, arrived at Kingsclere in 1964, just after Ian Balding took over the stable.

Second in the Cheveley Park, the One Thousand Guineas and the Oaks, poor Berkeley Springs was by nature a brides-maid rather than a bride and she has unfortunately carried on that tendency at stud. At her best though she was a top class filly and her older half-brother, Goose Creek, had already won four races, trained by Peter Hastings-Bass. Later, after winning twice over hurdles in America, Goose Creek stood at Rokeby and became the sire of Red Reef and Aldie, each of whom has a part to play in this story, and of the high-class steeplechaser, Tingle Creek. Thus, though, Milan Mill (Virginia Water's daughter by Princequillo) only managed to gain two minor placings as a two-year-old, it was by no means without hope that Paul Mellon retired her to his now rapidly developing stud.

That hope seemed justified when, in 1966, Milan Mill produced a colt by Never Bend called Milan Meadow. For two years later, when Milan Meadow began to work with contemporaries who included the brilliant Arts and Letters, Elliott Burch (Mr Mellon's trainer in America since 1962) considered him the best prospect of them all. That opinion was never tested because Milan Meadow broke down badly before he could run. But Milan Mill's great moment was now not long delayed. It came on the night of 23 February, 1968, when she was delivered of a bright bay foal whom Mr Mellon later named after a stretch of coastline near his winter home in Antigua.

The first human being Mill Reef saw that chilly night was George Comer, who has for many years had charge of Mr Mellon's mares, foals and yearlings at Rokeby. As George remembers it, there was nothing abnormal about the birth and Mill Reef was on his feet and suckling in less than normal time.

The lovely rolling stretch of Virginian countryside in which Milan Mill and her son were soon enjoying themselves had been bought by Paul Mellon's mother in 1931 and resold to him on his marriage in 1935. Since then, he has added to it the adjoining farms of Oak Spring, Loughborough and Milan Mill and the property now covers more than six thousand acres. Rokeby itself is as beautiful a stud as any in the world, a group of grey-and-white-painted stable yards set in six hundred acres of grassland dotted with woods of maple, sycamore, oak and gum and criss-crossed by quiet streams. A large red-brick house contains Mr Mellon's fabulous collection of paintings, books and sculptures, including among many other priceless works of art, some of the first books ever printed by Caxton and the original wax models for Degas's bronzes of ballet dancers and horses.

Here George Comer runs with loving care the nursery which, when Mill Reef was born, had already produced such great horses as Quadrangle, Arts and Letters and Fort Marcy.

His staff includes several of the huge gentle blacks on whom so much depends in American racing and breeding, and Howard White, a cheerful, voluble giant, always known as 'Boots', is inclined to claim that he was the first man ever to handle the young Mill Reef. He can certainly be seen holding him, as a yearling, in the picture facing page 33.

Much of the riding and breaking at Rokeby is now done by girls but the first human being ever to sit on Mill Reef's back was, like his trainer, a jumping jockey. Custer Cassidy is, in fact, a man of many parts for, besides riding winners over fences, he is a talented cartoonist whose work often appears in the *Chronicle of the Horse*.

They never drive the yearlings in long reins at Rokeby and after only a few days being saddled and led, the young colts and fillies are ridden loose, first in a covered barn, then round a sand track laid in one of the paddocks. According to Custer, Mill Reef was no trouble to break and his superlative action could be felt and seen from the beginning.

After two happy summers spent romping with his contemporaries (who included the subsequent Washington International winner, Run the Gantlet), Mill Reef was duly ridden away. And at about that time there took place a conference vital to his future.

It is only quite recently that Ian Balding has had much hand in deciding which of the Rokeby yearlings shall come to England and even now, understandably, Elliott Burch has first choice. In 1969, he, Mr Mellon and George Comer made the decision between them, and Elliott asked the advice of his father, Preston M. Burch, then retired after a long lifetime spent with horses and the author, incidentally, of one of the few good books about training ever written.

As the photograph opposite p. 33 shows, Mill Reef was an extremely attractive yearling, – much shorter coupled and more precocious-looking than he later became when in hard training. But as Mr Burch Senior had written in his book, 'long pasterns can be a source of unsoundness' – and it was this feature of the colt's anatomy which worried him now. Mill Reef's pasterns are indeed on the long side and quite possibly they might not have withstood much hammering on the hard dirt tracks of America. Anyway, it was agreed by all four men that English conditions would be more suitable, so Mill Reef joined Red Reef and Quantico in the Kingsclere consignment. At the time, Elliott Burch remembers, he most regretted the departure of Quantico, an exceptionally handsome and powerful colt by Graustark out of Blue Banner, a fine racemare herself and grandam of that wonderful indestructible gelding Fort Marcy.

Four years later, I was visiting Rokeby to gather material for this book when a Telex message arrived from Mrs Hastings: 'Quantico unplaced Stratford. Jockey satisfied'. The jockey may have been satisfied and Quantico did manage to win one hurdle race for Bob Turnell that winter. But his and Mill Reef's careers since they galloped together in the Rokeby paddocks are a sad confirmation of the fact that, whatever may be the case for human beings, horses are certainly not 'born equal'.

CHAPTER THREE

Kingsclere

Just over a hundred years before Mill Reef arrived at Kingsclere, John Porter lay in bed not far away at Cannon Heath recovering from typhoid fever. His chief patron, Sir Joseph Hawley, had already decided to build a new stable and, never a man to waste time, Porter called for a drawing board, T-square and paper, and began to draw up the plans. His chief worry at the time was that the drainage system connected with the pigsties and so anxious did he become about this that his doctor finally ordered him to 'forget those damned sties until you are better'.

Three years later, in 1868, Porter moved Sir Joseph's horses from Cannon Heath to Park House, Kingsclere, but although the pigsty problem had been solved, the move was not an immediate success. Porter's two best two-year-olds, Rosicrucian and Green Sleeve, both caught chills and the trainer, rightly or wrongly, blamed this disaster on the fact that the new boxes were still damp. Nowadays, no doubt, some virus would be held responsible, but whatever the cause, Rosicrucian, whom John Porter rated second only to Ormonde among all the good horses he trained, was still not fully recovered by Derby Day.

In a trial before Epsom, Rosicrucian did in fact manage to beat Sir Joseph's other good colt, Blue Gown, by a neck, but this news never reached the public because Porter had thoughtfully locked all the local touts in a toll-house where they had been carousing the night before. Probably, in his weakened state, the trial was too much for Rosicrucian, and Blue Gown won the Derby – to the delight of the punters who, disregarding his owner's declared preference for Rosicrucian and Green Sleeve, had made him second favourite at 7–2.

Blue Gown was the first of seven Derby winners John Porter trained at Kingsclere and in 1875, when Sir Joseph Hawley died, his will gave the trainer an option to buy Park House for £4,000, just half its original cost. After exercising this option, Porter spent a further £20,000 on developing and expanding the great red-brick yard to its present form.

For those who like footnotes to their history, it may be of interest that, during John Porter's long illness, Sir Joseph Hawley's horses were trained by a certain Jim Dover at West Ilsley, on the very gallops where, a century later, Brigadier Gerard first showed Dick Hern the power of his majestic stride.

John Porter, in fact, is buried in the churchyard in Kingsclere but at the highest point of Cannon Heath Down, a few hundred yards from the end of the seven furlong gallop, there is a square grey stone planted for purposes of their own by makers of the Ordnance Survey. When Geoff Lewis first rode out at Kingsclere, some mischievous stable-lad apparently told him that this was John Porter's grave-stone and Geoff has firmly believed it ever since.

'I nearly woke the old fellow this morning,' he would tell Ian Balding when Silly Season, a notoriously difficult horse to hold, had carried him past the end of the gallop. Ian did not disillusion him and although Geoff says that Mill Reef never got as far as the 'grave' it needs no undue stretch of imagination, I think, to see the great trainer's ghost astride his hack some misty summer morning, happy in the know-ledge that his beloved gallops were graced by a horse worthy to follow in Ormonde's footsteps.

Kingsclere has passed through various distinguished hands since John Porter's day, including those of Fred Butters, who trained Midday Sun there to win the 1937 Derby. But most of its masters had been experienced trainers until the summer of 1964 when, at the age of only twenty-six, Ian Balding took out a temporary licence on the death of Peter Hastings-Bass.

Earlier that year, already suffering from the illness that was to end his life so prematurely, Peter, who had bought Kingsclere from Evan Williams in 1953, felt the need of an assistant. Ian Balding had been helping both Herbert Blagrave at Beckhampton and his brother Toby at Fyfield, but his first love, even before Rugby football, was always the thrill of riding over fences and hurdles. He had already ridden seventy winners and, though pleased and proud to accept Peter Hastings-Bass's invitation, went to Kingsclere with no thought whatever of giving up his career as an amateur rider.

It was, accordingly, an agonising decision when, on her husband's death, Priscilla Hastings and the other Kingsclere owners asked him to carry on in sole command. A pointless and archaic rule of racing (soon I hope to be repealed) prohibits a licensed trainer from riding any but his own horses as an amateur. Nor was this Ian's only problem. For he, Toby and their mother had been building up Fyfield as a family business and to stay at Kingsclere meant opting out of that as well.

Not surprisingly, therefore, Ian asked for time to think and came very near indeed to saying 'No'. Among many things which influenced his decision, he remembers a conversation, while staying at Arundel, with the Duke of Edinburgh. Prince Philip, though no racing man, argued characteristically that England would soon be done for if her young men were not ready to take on heavy responsibilities early in life. As he put it, refusal would be playing safe, acceptance the only courageous course. Toby Balding had after all faced an even bigger challenge when taking over their father's stable at the age of twenty-one and so, half reluctantly, only too conscious of the risks involved, Ian decided to stay.

Thus it was that, five years later, one superlative natural athlete came under the control of another. For Ian Balding had won a Rugger Blue as full-back for Cambridge and if there is a game at which he does not excel, I have not seen him play it yet. Twice in his life he has ridden a winner and played top class Rugby on the same day, he came close to a second Blue for boxing and, whether as batsman, wicket-keeper or bowler, is a formidable addition to almost any cricket team.

But these athletic talents are only marginally a help in running a big flat race stable and Ian, great though his part was to be in Mill Reef's career, is only one of the men on whom that career depended.

Of a racehorse's waking life, a far greater proportion is spent in the company of the lad who does him than in that of any other human being. And in this respect as in so many others, Mill Reef was a lucky horse. John Hallum served his apprenticeship with Peter Nelson at Lambourn. But then, like so many others who are prevented by weight or lack of opportunity from making the grade as a jockey, he drifted out of racing altogether and took a job as a machine operator in Doncaster.

It was not a bad job as they go, but the route from John's house to his place of work led past Doncaster Racecourse and served as a constant nagging reminder of another very different life. So, finally, about the time Ian Balding was making one difficult decision, John Hallum and his wife made another, and John applied for a job at Kingsclere. The trainer cannot have been long in recognising his merits because, soon after arriving, he was given charge of a four-year-old gelding called Morris Dancer. And 'Morris', though now the doyen and darling of the yard, has never been exactly a child's pony to handle. His foibles include pulling like a runaway omnibus – and chasing out of the box any stranger rash enough to venture there. But John Hallum's arms were always equal to the first challenge and the old horse long ago made him an exception to the second. As one of the senior lads in 1969, John was given his pick of Mr Mellon's yearlings. And, providentially rejecting the massive good looks of Quantico, he chose Mill Reef. So there began a friendship which only ended in the spring of 1973 when, with a heavy heart, John Hallum said goodbye in the yard of the National Stud at Newmarket.

In the four intervening years, he rode Mill Reef almost every day of his life, travelled with him to all his fourteen races, groomed him for countless hours and nursed him devotedly through his final tribulations. No other man had better reason to love the little horse and no one who ever saw them together can doubt the extent to which that love was wholeheartedly returned.

A trainer, they say, is only as good as his head lad and although there are exceptions to that rule, Ian Balding makes no claim to be one of them. So it was a crucial landmark in his and Mill Reef's life when Bill Palmer came from Fyfield to take over on the retirement of Peter Hastings-Bass's head lad, Charlie Moore.

It was a reunion of almost lifelong friends, for Bill and Ian had, since their early teens, been brought up together. Bill was apprenticed to Ian's father and, since the latter's death, had both worked and ridden regularly for his brother Toby. When Ian began to succeed as an amateur, the two of them must often have been in direct competition for rides but to their common credit, there was never a trace of the jealousy which so often embitters such situations.

In 1969, in fact, although Bill had hung up his boots the previous year, it was a generous brotherly gesture on Toby's part to release so fine a stableman. But he had both a head lad and a travelling lad of his own and realised that there was no job at Fyfield comparable with the one now vacant at Kingsclere. So Bill and Anne Palmer moved into the little house behind the mess room John Porter built for his stable lads and a happy working partnership began which, in the next two seasons, turned out a total of ninety-five winners.

'We speak the same language, Bill and I,' Ian says. 'If I'm away, I never have a moment's worry. I *know* things will be done just as if I was there.'

The team on whose skill and care Mill Reef's success depended had many other members, notably Ian's travelling head lad, Bill Jennings, who, except for the horse's first race at Salisbury, was in charge of all his journeys. Paul Cook and Philip Waldron both rode him in a good deal of work at home and almost every lad in the yard, down to the youngest apprentice, played a willing part in the final drama of his life at Kingsclere.

Ian Balding only takes on three carefully selected apprentices each year and, unlike some trainers, makes a real effort both to teach them their job and, having done so, to get them rides in public. Ernie Johnson, and Philip Waldron, now the stable jockey, are the most successful products of his efforts so far, but John Matthias is already showing comparable promise.

A training stable is like a machine. It can run rough or smooth and the oil which keeps it turning is a compound of the trainer's personality and his relationship with his employees. At Kingsclere, that relationship, securely based on the close understanding between Ian Balding and Bill Palmer, is a supremely happy one. So in this respect too, Mill Reef – whose coming made it happier still – was fortunate indeed.

CHAPTER FOUR

Salisbury and Ascot

Rumour spreads even faster on the racecourse than the equine flu' bug and the day before Nijinsky was due to run in the 1970 Two Thousand Guineas everyone at Newmarket from the senior steward to the bootboy at The Rutland Arms seemed to know about a flying two-year-old called Fireside Chat. Mr Charles Engelhard, or rather his trainer Fulke Johnson-Houghton, had bought Fireside Chat at the January Hialeah sales, an auction remarkable for the fact that some of the two-year-olds sold there are publicly galloped – and clocked – before they enter the sale ring. Fireside Chat's deportment in this commercial kindergarten had made him look worth 80,000 dollars and, since arriving at Blewbury he had, so the story went, been making the Berkshire pigeons fly for their lives.

The intrepid punters who, acting confidently on the strength of this information, made Fireside Chat a 6–5 favourite for the first race on Guineas Day were somewhat perturbed to see him lurch clumsily out of the stalls at least ten lengths behind his more wide awake opponents. At half way his position was still a long way from that recommended for short priced favourites in five furlong races and I for one had begun to think harshly of the dream-merchant who had told me so emphatically that 'this one could fall down twice and still win'.

But my informant was not, as it turned out, all that far wrong. In the last two furlongs, balanced and galvanised by

Lester Piggott, Fireside Chat suddenly lived right up to his advance billing. He passed a dozen horses as though they were going the other way and, catching Double Dare two hundred yards from home, won by four rapidly expanding lengths.

It was by any standards a deeply impressive performance and since everybody likes being proved right, especially when their pockets are involved, quite a large number of people left Newmarket convinced, not only that they had spotted Fireside Chat's excellence all by themselves but also that he must be the fastest two-year-old in training. So when he reappeared at Salisbury a fortnight later you could scarcely blame the bookmakers for framing a market designed to discourage all but the very boldest. Nine to two on Fireside Chat and 8–1 bar one was the cry, and it pains me to record that not very many punters took advantage of what, in retrospect, looks one of the most attractive offers since the impressionists were peddling their pictures for the price of a drink along the Seine.

Because for once the bookmakers' sensitive antennae – which are usually tuned to pick up news of promising two-year-olds long before they see a racecourse – had fallen down on the job.

By the first week in May no Kingsclere two-year-old had run in public and none in fact had done more than swing along on the bit at what is often called 'a good half speed'. Though as an experienced trainer said to me one morning as we watched some pretty moderate animals cruise past, 'the trouble about half-speed gallops begins when you try to find the other half'.

In those early carefree jaunts Mill Reef's enthusiasm and superlative action were already evident. But Ian Balding had been a trainer quite long enough to know how full the form book is of superlative movers who cannot, when it comes to the crunch, go fast enough to catch a number 19 bus. He therefore decided, having chosen the Salisbury Stakes for

Mill Reef's initiation, to let him stretch his legs just once in real earnest. The question then arose of a suitable galloping companion and after some discussion with Bill Palmer Ian chose Red Reef, a nice grey colt by Mill Reef's maternal uncle Goose Creek. Red Reef in fact never ran as a two-year-old owing to a split pastern and needed both time and distance to reach his potential. But he was quite highly thought of at the time, notably by the lad who did him, Joe Bonner.

So poor Joe was even more surprised – and somewhat less delighted – than Ian Balding by what happened early on the morning of Saturday 9 May. John Hallum's orders had been 'let him lead you to the bend and then come on together'. But at the bend Mill Reef was still lobbing contentedly two lengths behind his cousin and John remembers thinking, 'Well, if you're ever going to be any good you've got to do something now.' So, without much confidence in the outcome he changed his grip on the reins and slapped Mill Reef down the neck. It was the first time anyone had asked that sort of question and the answer was emphatic. In just over a furlong, without coming off a tight rein, Mill Reef opened up a lead of between twenty and thirty lengths.

Apart from actually winning the Derby or some other longed-for prize a moment like this must be as near perfect happiness as any in a trainer's life. There is of course always the possibility of a fluke – and to beat Red Reef, good horse though he later became, was not exactly a Herculean achievement. But Ian Balding had seen the whole gallop. He knew how late John Hallum had allowed Mill Reef to go and how little time there had been to build up such a lead. Walking downhill behind the string he tried very hard to be coldly realistic, to question and qualify the evidence of his eyes. But even then, making all possible allowances he still found himself convinced – and has never since had reason to change his mind – that this was far and away the best performance he had ever seen at Kingsclere by a two-year-old of Mill Reef's tender age and comparative inexperience.

The news of the work did not leak out, and for Geoff Lewis, who had never so far ridden Mill Reef, the following Wednesday was just another working day. He had rides in all six races at Salisbury and walked out for the third in the familiar black and gold colours with no particularly special feeling of excitement.

It is not Ian Balding's custom to over-test his two-year-olds in the starting stalls and although Mill Reef had been walking through them almost all his life he had only once been asked to jump out in earnest at racing pace. The result had been a clumsy fiasco and, finding him drawn at No. 1 at Salisbury, on the wide outside of an eleven horse field, Ian warned Geoff to expect a slow beginning. Lester Piggott on Fireside Chat were drawn No. 7 much nearer the rails so the plan agreed on was to drop in behind them and hope for the best. 'But mind you,' said Ian, 'this is a nice colt. You might just find yourself bustling him up towards the end.'

What neither trainer nor jockey then appreciated was that Mill Reef is among other things a quite exceptionally quick learner. Again and again throughout his life a nod has been as good as a wink and the first public demonstration of this priceless attribute was to be the start of the Salisbury Stakes. That one lesson at Kingsclere had taught Mill Reef all that any racehorse needs to know about the starting stalls. When they open the back you go in and when they open the front you come out fast. 'One moment he'll be standing there half asleep,' Geoff Lewis says now, 'the next, you'd better hang on tight'.

In fact, exploding out of the gate like a veteran sprinter, Mill Reef was clear in front after a hundred yards. A surprised and delighted Geoff Lewis felt able to come across towards the rails – though some observers, notably L. Piggott and the Salisbury Stewards, thought he did so rather sooner than was prudent! But it made not the remotest difference. Before half-way Fireside Chat was struggling in vain pursuit

and, storming gaily home four lengths in front Geoff Lewis
had time to give Mill Reef one of those huge triumphant
slaps which, on other more famous occasions were to become
the familiar mark of his delight.

An interview with the Stewards followed – at which Lester
was not exactly counsel for the defence. 'You're *always* doing
it,' he said afterwards – but Geoff was far too happy to argue.
On dismounting he had already told Ian Balding, 'This is
the best you've ever had – or ever *will* have', and he, like
the trainer, has had no reason to alter that view.

Ian's travelling head lad Bill Jennings was at York that
day and so, with John Hallum detailed to take his place, Joe
Bonner had charge of Mill Reef. They, Bill Palmer and Mrs
Hastings seem to have been the only ones at Kingsclere who
took advantage of the 8–1 available for the Salisbury Stakes –
which was a pity. Because Mill Reef was never again to
start at anything like such generous odds.

There was just over a month between Salisbury and Royal
Ascot and, as he was to do again next year, Mill Reef made
more physical progress in that period than at any other part
of the season. After ten days rest he galloped regular as
clockwork twice a week and the comments on Ian Balding's
work sheets are brief but eloquent. 'Very strong', 'cantering',
'very impressive' and 'easily best'. That last one meant most
for it followed a six furlong gallop with Morris Dancer –
already nine years old it is true but full (as he still is) of
beans and well on his way to winning more prize money than
any gelding in British racing history.

The 'valley' gallop at Kingsclere runs, as its name suggests
along the floor of a winding fold in the Downs. Sheltered on
either side and uphill all the way it provides both superlative
summer going and an extremely searching test. Ian Balding
is the only trainer I know who has tried out the relative
stiffness of all his gallops by *running* them himself. It is not
a method that could be safely recommended to many of his
colleagues but one which has obvious advantages. And one

The first painting Mr Mellon can remember: Miss Willoughby, by Romney

Mr Mellon on Dublin, by Sir Alfred Munnings PRA

As a yearling

As a two-
year-old

As a three-year-old

of the lessons it taught Ian is that only a truly exceptional athlete has much in reserve after six furlongs up the valley. But Mill Reef finished pulling Geoff Lewis' arms out and by that time Morris Dancer, giving him only a stone – twenty-eight pounds less than normal weight-for-age – had decided long ago that youth could have its day. Morris Dancer had always been a particularly good worker at home and it is largely on the basis of this gallop that Ian Balding rates Mill Reef as much as 21 lb. better than Silly Season at the same stage of his career. And Silly Season, though just beaten by Double Jump at Salisbury, went on to win the Coventry Stakes.

So to say that the stable approached Royal Ascot with confidence would be an understatement. Their only doubt was whether the bookies would let them bet and in fact, with only four opponents, Mill Reef started at 11–4 on. That's hardly a working man's price with betting tax to pay but the five runners had not been in the Ascot paddock long before a steady stream of determined looking punters was to be seen marching across the Royal Enclosure towards Tattersalls' rails as though a free issue of diamonds had just been announced.

They looked like people who had seen a marvel – and they had. For no lover of horses, or indeed of beauty in any form, will easily forget his first sight of Mill Reef at Royal Ascot. With the possible exception of the 1971 Eclipse I do not believe he ever again came quite so near to physical perfection.

Though always superbly balanced and with quality etched in every line he often tended afterwards to run up light behind the saddle in hard training. But at Ascot his middle piece was so deep and his quarters so round that no lack of scope was apparent. Under the gleaming mahogany coat the muscles of his forearms and second thighs rippled like sleepy snakes and as he danced light-footed round the tree lined paddock, long ears cocked to the unfamiliar sights and sounds, the blend of explosive power with easy natural grace was unforgettable.

Only one of the other four runners, the Crepello colt Cromwell, had previous winning form and he was quite unable to make the Coventry Stakes anything but a triumphal progress. Clear at half way Mill Reef drew relentlessly further and further ahead and passed the post pulling so hard that Geoff Lewis could not contrive to stop him for fully another quarter of a mile.

The time, 1 m. 16.16 s., was just over a second slower than the six furlong record for a two-year-old set in 1957 by Amerigo. Welsh Pageant and Connaught had broken the mile and ten furlong records earlier that same day and there cannot be much doubt I think that, with something to extend him even slightly, Mill Reef would have followed their example. As things were he went home to Kingsclere scarcely knowing that he had had a race and was back on the gallops eight days later earning from his trainer the satisfied comment 'keen and well'.

But that very afternoon as Mill Reef dozed unconcernedly in his box, a big bay colt caused quite a stir six miles down the road at Newbury. He won the Berkshire Stakes very easily indeed and his name was Brigadier Gerard.

CHAPTER FIVE

Defeat

Two years before Mill Reef arrived at Kingsclere, Ian Balding had won both the Salisbury and Coventry Stakes with a colt called Murrayfield, owned by his mother-in-law, Priscilla Hastings. But although Murrayfield later won five races in Italy, his English career had been relatively unfruitful after Ascot; now, largely because of that disappointment, Mill Reef's was planned on very different lines.

Pedigrees – and the too-strict interpretation of their significance – have a good deal to answer for in racing. The root cause of Murrayfield's troubles, for instance, was that, being by Match III out of a Doutelle mare, he was in theory bred to win a Derby and certainly not to be a precociously fast two-year-old. But in fact, though he ran really well to be fourth in Right Tack's Two Thousand Guineas, Murrayfield did not really stay much beyond a mile. Speed was his strongest weapon and, having wasted it, in the second half of his two-year-old career, in races designed for potential stayers like the Solario and Royal Lodge Stakes, Ian Balding determined not to make the same mistake again.

Anyone lucky enough nowadays to own a top-class two-year-old faces an almost irresistible temptation to run him or her in France. I say 'almost' because Mr and Mrs John Hislop always firmly refused to send Brigadier Gerard across the Channel. But the price they had to pay for their sporting patriotism (on the short term at least) can be seen from a comparison of the Brigadier's two-year-old earnings (£13,467

in four races, of which the Middle Park accounted for
£10,515) with those of My Swallow. No less than four times
in five separate journeys to France, My Swallow earned (in
one race) more than the Brigadier's entire total. And the last
of his triumphs, the £34,724 Grand Criterium, brought his
haul for the season to a record £88,355. There is absolutely
no doubt, however, which of those pounds – or rather francs
– were the most difficult to earn. And if My Swallow had
never done anything else, his victory in the Prix Robert
Papin will alone have assured him a place in this story.

With not a single worthwhile English prize available between Ascot and York, this was the next target chosen by
Ian Balding for Mill Reef. The Prix Robert Papin was run
at Maisons-Laffitte on Monday 20 July and the moment the
plan was announced, several normally hard-working and
conscientious persons of my acquaintance decided that this
particular week-end would have to be extended, even if it
meant suffering a serious stomach upset or killing off a
grandmother for the purpose.

These things are easier for racing correspondents and,
having obtained permission to cover the race, my only problem was to acquire sufficient local currency with which to
back Mill Reef as he deserved. For some obscure Gallic
reason, all the banks were closed in Paris that Monday
morning but American Express eventually came up trumps
and, hailing a taxi outside the Ritz, I asked the driver with
misplaced confidence to take me *aux courses*.

It was quite some time and several phrasebooks later that
the awful truth began to dawn. The *courses* for which the
evil-tempered driver had been searching so ineffectually
turned out to be Saint-Cloud and that, as my map of *les
environs* told me, is a longish way from Maisons-Laffitte.

Looking back now, I half wish we had never reached
journey's end at all, but at the time, no thirsty desert traveller
ever greeted an oasis more fervently than I the course gates.
There was almost an hour to spare and, hurrying towards

the *pari-mutuel* windows, I encountered another welcome
sight, the cheerful bespectacled face of John Ciechanowski.

There is a whole book to be written about John and his
career, starting in Poland, which he left in 1939 one hurried
step ahead of the German army, continuing with his strenuous
efforts to avenge that inconvenience, and ending triumphantly
with a sixth in the Grand National, a European Amateur
Riders' Championship at over forty – and with more friends
on both sides of the Channel than any other man I know.

For the moment, however, knowing that he had not been
at Royal Ascot, my only desire was to let him in on a good
thing. So I invited him to 'come and see the most beautiful
two-year-old in the world', and together we walked into the
pretty stable yard which at Maisons serves as a sort of pre-
parade ring.

The first horse to go by was a massive gleaming bay whom
I did not immediately recognise.

'Well, yes,' said John. 'Yes, I see what you mean.'

I was just about to explain that Mill Reef had not yet
appeared when a small doleful figure walked rather hesitantly
out of a nearby box. It was the worst moment yet of an
already far-from-perfect day.

For this listless half-starved little creature bore no re-
semblance whatever to the resplendent winner of the
Coventry Stakes. Mill Reef was almost unrecognisable and,
beside My Swallow – the bay John Ciechanowski had so
understandably admired – he looked, more than anything
else, like a suitable case for treatment by the RSPCA.

Three days earlier, leaving Kingsclere for Eastleigh Airport,
near Southampton, Mill Reef, perhaps for the first time in
his life, had been bandaged as a precaution on his hind legs
as well as his front ones. For some unknown reason, he took
violent exception to this measure and from that moment on,
behaved quite unlike his usual placid self. A long wait at
the airport did not help, nor did the journey by horse-box
from Le Bourget to Maisons-Laffitte. Most French horse-box

drivers approach their work with more regard for speed than the convenience of their passengers.

Arriving at last in the racecourse stables, Mill Reef, who is normally a voracious eater, refused to touch his evening feed. For twenty-four hours he ate nothing at all and, after passing a stalls test on Saturday, left more than half his dinner again that night. By Sunday evening, he had still not finished a single meal and, although he was then beginning at last to settle down, it seems fairly safe to guess that he had slept and rested far less than usual. Certainly no one who saw him, tucked up and miserable on Monday afternoon, would quarrel with Ian Balding's view that, in those four days, he had lost at least forty pounds in weight.

Travelling, of course, is part of a racehorse's life and nerves are something every champion has to overcome. My Swallow was just as far from home and deserves full credit for any advantage his own mental and physical toughness gave him. But nerves and the journey were not Mill Reef's only handicap. He also had the worst possible draw – No. 9 in a field of that number – and My Swallow (drawn No. 1) had the best.

To make matters worse, Geoff Lewis had not then fully appreciated Mill Reef's ability to come from behind. He had not been headed in either of his first two races and, not surprisingly, Geoff hoped to jump off sharp and come across towards the rails as he had at Salisbury. But, drawn on his immediate left, number seven in fact, was a fast colt called Tarbes who, as a three-year-old, won the Prix Lupin and finished second in the French Two Thousand Guineas. And now, quickly though Mill Reef broke from the stalls, Tarbes broke even quicker. His jockey, mindful no doubt of the French stewards' puritanical attitude to such things, made no attempt to alter course and so, after two furlongs, Geoff Lewis found himself, to his horror, still nine horses wide of the rail up which My Swallow was racing.

For the first time in his life, Mill Reef was well and truly off the bit and at halfway, their prospects even of gaining a place seemed to his rider very slim.

'So I gave him a quick backhander,' Geoff says, 'and suddenly, without really knowing how, we were upsides in front.' But almost the whole width of the course still lay between them and My Swallow and, in drifting across towards his rival over the next half furlong, Mill Reef had to waste both ground and precious energy.

Nevertheless, he was still a yard or so in front with a furlong left and there followed, I believe, an episode as brave as any in his whole career. Throughout that last furlong, drawing steadily clear of the French, he and My Swallow fought out a desperate duel, with Mill Reef clinging to his huge opponent like a terrier at a bulldog's throat. Neither jockey spared his mount and it was noticeable, in fact, that both went on riding flat out fully ten yards past the line.

While the photograph was being developed, almost all the local experts felt that Mill Reef had won, but both Geoff and Lester Piggott thought otherwise.

'I knew I had him ten yards out,' the champion told Peter O'Sullevan, adding a well-deserved tribute to My Swallow : 'A real tough one – he has a right go.'

The ground at Maisons, heavily watered in advance, had been further softened by rain over-night and in the unsaddling enclosure afterwards, Mill Reef was a picture of exhaustion. As he walked wearily away, Ladbrokes' representative bracketed him and My Swallow as 7–1 favourites for the next year's Two Thousand Guineas. But I do not suppose I was the only one of his admirers present who wondered pessimistically if he would ever be quite the same after this singularly gruelling ordeal.

Deep under the grandstand at Maisons-Laffitte, there is a candle-lit cellar in which jockeys, ex-jockeys and their hangers-on gather to drink and discuss the doings of the day. John Ciechanowski kindly took me there to drown my sorrows in champagne and a long argument was raging over the Papin result. Most of it, my feeble French could not decipher, but there was one old man, a wrinkled brown-faced veteran, who had, they told me, ridden Ksar and must therefore have been seventy or more. *'Le Petit'*, he kept saying, *'Le Petit – mon Dieu, quel cheval – quel coeur.'* Even I could understand that and it seemed as good an epilogue as any to Mill Reef's first defeat.

CHAPTER SIX

The Gimcrack

Late at night 19 August, 1970, Ian Balding, who normally sleeps like a hibernating bear, was anxiously pacing the floor of his bedroom a few miles outside York. Since early evening, the rain had been streaming down and in an hotel not far away, it was keeping Geoff Lewis awake too – by splashing into the river outside his window. The same gloomy thoughts were in both their minds – for York racecourse is not called the Knavesmire for nothing and the last thing Mill Reef needed at that stage of his career was another hard race in heavy ground.

The Gimcrack Stakes, due to be run next day, had seemed for several reasons to fit ideally into his programme. My Swallow had been announced a runner for the more valuable French alternative, the Prix Morny, and, quite apart from the obvious desirability of postponing another head-on collision with him, Mr Mellon, whose long-time friend, Lord Halifax, is president of 'Ye Anciente Fraternite of York Gimcracks', was keen to support the club in this, the two-hundredth year of its existence.

But now, it seemed, the rain was going to spoil everything. Geoff Lewis's impression at Maisons-Laffitte had been that Mill Reef could not get a proper grip on the heavily-watered ground and although the little horse had not left a single oat uneaten since that race, it still seemed entirely possible that the experience might have left a lasting mark.

Walking down the stand side of the six furlong course on

the morning of the Gimcrack, Ian Balding's worst fears were justified. Deep hoof-prints from the previous day's racing were rapidly filling with water and by the time he arrived at the start, Ian had made up his mind that to run in such conditions would be not only foolish but downright dangerous. At that point, however, he met the assistant starter and was told that the stewards had already decided to place the starting stalls for the straight races on the far side of the course. Walking back along that rail, he found a definite improvement, but the ground was still far softer than anything Mill Reef had ever galloped, let alone raced on.

Left to himself at this stage, Ian would almost certainly have withdrawn there and then, but now for the first time Mr Mellon had come from America to see Mill Reef run. Having gloomily reported the situation to his owner in the Halifa'x box, Ian suggested that they should at least wait until Geoff Lewis had ridden in the first race of the day.

So around 2.15 that afternoon, less than an hour before declaration time for the Gimcrack, the three men met in the glass-fronted weighing room at York. Geoff's verdict was emphatic.

'I've never ridden on softer ground in all my life,' he said, and added that if, despite everything, they did decide to run, he would like permission, whatever happened, not to use his whip.

Mr Mellon turned to Ian.

'What would you do if I weren't here?'

'I'm afraid I'd certainly withdraw.'

There was a pause after that and then Mr Mellon said quietly, 'Well, I just have a feeling everything will be all right and that we should run.' He readily gave Geoff the permission he had asked for and assured Ian that the decision had nothing to do with his own presence at York, with the Gimcrack Club or with anything else apart from the horse's welfare.

'I just have this feeling,' he repeated; 'Everything will be all right.'

So trainer and jockey went off about their business – not exactly happy perhaps, but at least with considerable loads off their minds. For Geoff indeed it was in a way the perfect set-up – nothing much to lose and no need to persevere and overstrain Mill Reef if it turned out (as both he and Ian expected) that he could not handle the mud.

There were seven other runners in the Gimcrack Stakes and they had already won fourteen races between them. One, King's Company, went on to win the Irish Two Thousand Guineas and the Cork and Orrery Stakes the following year, and exactly twelve months later another, the second favourite, Green God, was to finish first in the Nunthorpe Stakes at York. Although disqualified that day, he also won the Vernons Sprint and four other races and had a better claim than any other horse to the title of Champion Sprinter in 1971. So the dream-like sequence of events which now ensued cannot be explained by writing off the opposition.

Geoff Lewis's recipe for riding in heavy ground is that once a horse has settled to his stride, you should never take him out of it. Accordingly, he let Mill Reef choose his own pace and four horses, Trem Blay, King's Company, Most Secret and Green God, were a length or so in front of him until half way. There Geoff took stock of the position.

'Frankie [Durr] was riding the ears off Green God,' he says. 'All the others I could see were dead meat – and here am I, just barely going half speed. There didn't seem much point in giving them a second chance, so I let him run for half a furlong. And when I looked round – well, it was unbelievable.'

It was indeed, for in that half furlong, without coming off the bit, Mill Reef had gone four or five lengths clear. Long before the end, Geoff started pulling up – or meant to any-way – but at the line the verdict was still ten lengths. And

43

later, when Ian Balding said jokingly to the judge, John Hancock, 'That didn't test your eyesight too severely,' John replied that, oddly enough, it had been a very difficult distance to assess : 'Because even at the post, your fellow was still going so much faster than the others that, in another hundred yards, he'd have won by twenty lengths, not ten.'

Not surprisingly, this wholesale massacre generated a cloudburst of superlatives from the racing press. Opinions given in the heat and excitement of the day are apt to be exaggerated but although one may not always agree with them, Phil Bull's 'Timeform' experts can usually be relied on for an objective considered view in their annual survey *Racehorses*. And, after calling the Gimcrack 'far the most impressive display by a two-year-old all season', they added that 'a literal interpretation of the result – Mill Reef gave the runner-up, Green God, a 33 lb. beating – would have made him the best two-year-old we have ever seen !'

Inevitably, and no doubt to some extent justifiably, *Racehorses of 1970* hastened to qualify that interpretation by suggesting the probability that Mill Reef was 'the only one of the principals really suited by the ground'. That may well have been so and I merely note in passing that a year later, *Racehorses of 1971* not only described the ground as 'heavy' when King's Company won at Royal Ascot, but also ended its commentary on Green God with the words 'acts on any going'.

But anyway, even if Mill Reef's opponents in the Gimcrack were handicapped more than he by the conditions, that is in itself surely a glowing testimonial to the versatility of a horse who, next season, was to win the Eclipse Stakes by six lengths in record time on going officially described as 'firm'.

'Great horses act on any ground' is a saying that can be interpreted in many ways. For instance, Brigadier Gerard certainly could act on soft ground – and did so well enough to win a St James's Palace, a Champion and an Eclipse

Stakes. Clearly, however, as the results of those and his other races prove, he was a far more formidable proposition on good or even firm going. There have in fact been very few horses indeed, great or otherwise, who were equally good whatever the conditions. Arkle was one who springs to mind and, beyond argument I think, Mill Reef was another.

It is a shattering thought that, but for Mr Mellon's bold decision (based on nothing more concrete than 'a feeling'), this crucial fact might never have been known. For caution leads to caution and if Mill Reef had been withdrawn from the Gimcrack, the rest of his career would most likely have been charted to avoid soft ground. In fact he only once again faced comparable conditions – in his first race as a four-year-old, the Prix Ganay at Longchamp. And without his spreadeagling victory that day, there would have been no evidence of what I firmly believe to be the truth, namely, that he went on improving throughout his career and was at least as good in the spring of 1972 as at any previous time.

It was long after the Gimcrack in fact that Ian Balding found at least a partial answer to the question of how a horse with Mill Reef's flawless, feather-light action could contrive not to be thrown out of gear by the sort of quagmire he encountered at York.

On the morning before the 1971 Prix de l'Arc de Triomphe, Mill Reef and his travelling companion Aldie did a four-and-a-half furlong pipe-opener up a strip of watered gallop near their stables at Lamorlaye. The going was mostly good, except for two or three soft patches. Walking down the gallop afterwards, Ian could see quite clearly where Aldie's hooves had printed the turf, but of Mill Reef's passage there was no sign until he reached the first soft patch. And there the difference was even more glaringly apparent. For while Aldie, a firm ground specialist with a low sweeping action, had cut in three or four inches deep and actually turned the turf over, Mill Reef's small feet had only barely left a mark.

Since that day, his fascinated trainer noticed the same phenomenon many times and so did Jona Holley, the man who lovingly cares for the gallops at Kingsclere.

'It's as though a ghost had galloped by,' says Ian and although neither he nor I had ever heard of such a thing before, there does not seem to be much doubt that some quality in Mill Reef's action enabled him to float where others sank and fly where they could only flounder.

Probably, like most exceptional athletes, his excellence in this respect depended more on timing than strength. And it would be no easier to analyse his action at full stretch than Gary Sobers's on-drive, Barry John's sidestep or the back-hand of Ken Rosewall. All you can say for certain is that these were things of beauty – and that their results are on the scoreboard.

CHAPTER SEVEN

Imperial and Dewhurst

When Mill Reef arrived to start life as a stallion at the National Stud in 1973 his masculine prowess was first tested on a comparatively humble mare called Village Gossip, bought specially for the purpose. (She was not, at that stage, allowed to conceive but Mr Mellon later decided that she had earned the honour of a second less abortive mating.)

Of the other twenty-two carefully chosen concubines who made up his limited harem for the first season the earliest to arrive was an elegant bay mare called Hecla. And Mill Reef whether he remembered it or not had met her before in very different, rather less romantic circumstances. Apart from My Swallow in fact Hecla was the only two-year-old in the whole of 1970 who ever looked remotely like beating him.

Delighted though he was with Mill Reef's performance in the Gimcrack, Ian Balding still purposely refrained from looking too far ahead. But the Two Thousand Guineas was now clearly a very real possibility and as a dress rehearsal for it he chose the seven furlong Dewhurst Stakes in preference to the shorter Middle Park. There was time for one more race between York and Newmarket though, and the valuable Imperial Stakes at Kempton looked a nice juicy plum ripe for easy picking on the way. But not for the first time in racing history pride – or anyway slight over-confidence – very nearly came before a fall.

For, having understandably given Mill Reef a good rest after the Gimcrack, Ian frankly admits to having regarded

47

the Imperial Stakes more as a public tune-up for the Dewhurst than as a serious test in its own right. When he went to Kempton Mill Reef had done no really serious gallop since York and, always a horse who thrives on hard work, his appearance left a good deal to be desired.

So, I am afraid, did his behaviour because, startled by an umbrella on his way to the parade ring, he plunged violently away from John Hallum. For several hectic moments it was touch and go whether John would be able to hold him at all and by the time peace was restored both horse and man had scared themselves half out of their wits. This was not in fact the first or the last time that Mill Reef's pre-race deportment fell below his usual high standards. He had been frightened before the Gimcrack – by those boards which give the York crowd such up-to-date betting news around the paddock – and much the same was to happen next year before the Guineas.

At the time at Kempton however it seemed of little consequence. Of Mill Reef's five opponents only Hecla had anything like top-class form and she had been beaten at Ascot the previous month. How could she possibly be expected to trouble an effortless winner of races like the Coventry and Gimcrack? Well, to that question Hecla and her young South African jockey John Gorton soon produced their answer. Out of the gate like a scalded cat, the filly still led Mill Reef by more than a length at half way and suddenly as Geoff Lewis began to ride, there came from the Kempton crowd that peculiar sound, half buzz, half groan which means that the impossible – or at least the unforeseeable – is about to happen on a racecourse.

That it did not quite happen was due to a combination of Geoff Lewis's strength and Mill Reef's willing co-operation. Though just for a moment the latter looked in doubt. 'He hung fire for a bit when I first asked him' Geoff remembers 'as if he was saying, "Oh Lord, what are you getting at *now*?" But in the end he got the message.'

The Gimcrack

Defeat by Brigadier Gerard in the Two Thousand Guineas

The Derby finish

And a slap for the winner

The message was conveyed both urgently and dexterously a furlong out as Geoff pulled the whip through to his left hand and welded it quite sharply twice. A hundred and fifty yards from the line the whole picture was transformed and, brushing poor Hecla aside Mill Reef won going steadily away. He only won by a length, however, and had taken an unconscionable time to do so. There were plenty of critics who saw the beginning of the end in this rather undignified scramble – the sad inevitable splutter of a brilliant shooting-star, too hot not to cool down.

But there was of course an alternative explanation and now, looking back, we can see that it was probably the right one. For Mill Reef was never just a precocious flying machine. He was much more than that and even at this stage of his career six furlongs on a sharp track and fast ground scarcely gave him time to hoist full sail. He was also undoubtedly short of work at Kempton and when he got back to Kingsclere one of his fetlock joints was found to be sore and bruised, probably as a result of those antics in the paddock.

Having said all that I am sure that Mill Reef himself would be the first to give Hecla her due share of credit. She was a very fast filly as well as a very pretty one and if their off-spring has a leg at each corner and even half its parents' character I shall take some persuading to bet much money against it.

Anyone in whose mind the Kempton race left serious doubts about Mill Reef's future had less than a month to wait for reassurance. Because he not only looked his old self in the paddock before the Dewhurst Stakes but also won the race with every bit as much authority as Nijinsky had the year before.

The two Irish colts Wenceslas and Lombardo who made up the opposition had each won his previous race and Lombardo was to train on into a very useful three-year-old. But at Newmarket on 16 October, 1970 both he and Wenceslas were comprehensively cut down to size. Though

singularly lacking in suspense and excitement as a race the
Dewhurst was for Mill Reef a useful tactical exercise. Because
here for the first time Geoff Lewis expressly set out to ride
him from behind. And no seasoned three mile chaser could
have settled more calmly behind his two opponents.

From the dip, however, it was they who looked like three
mile chasers and as Mill Reef scampered up the hill four
lengths in front of Wenceslas Geoff had not once found it
necessary to change his grip on the reins. No horse could have
had a happier end to his first season and I for one went
home from Newmarket convinced that, barring accidents, the
result of the 1971 Two Thousand Guineas was as good as in
the form book. Which was of course ridiculous, for only five
days before the Dewhurst My Swallow had rounded off an
even more triumphant year by winning the Grand Criterium
at Longchamps. Ten days earlier Brigadier Gerard had won
his fourth and most impressive victory in the Middle Park
Stakes, slamming fast horses like Mummy's Pet, Swing Easy
and Mill Reef's old rival Fireside Chat. And although
Nijinsky's great career was to end on a downward note the
day after the Dewhurst there were those in Ireland who
claimed that his full brother Minsky was getting ready to
start where he left off.

So as Mill Reef returned to Kingsclere for his winter
holiday the stage was set for a confrontation as full of
fascinating possibilities as any in the long history of the Two
Thousand Guineas.

CHAPTER EIGHT

At Home

Only a tiny fraction of a horse's life is spent on the race-course and behind the fleeting public moments of triumph or disaster there lie long private hours in which only a handful of human beings are involved. But a thoroughbred colt is such an explosive, unpredictable and perishable property that no single one of those hours is free from risk. And in Mill Reef's life, despite his basically placid temperament there were several moments which no one present will easily forget.

After Royal Ascot, for instance, Ian Balding gave him ten days rest and, one sunny morning sent John Hallum along with two fillies and a hack, for a quiet amble round the paths and hedgerows. Ian himself went off to supervise the morning work and told John to meet him at the sand gallop which runs round a paddock near the stables. It was here, by custom, that the string used to stop on the way back from exercise – to pick grass and, on fine days have a roll in the sand. Mill Reef was especially fond of rolling and as Ian arrived in the paddock that morning John Hallum had just taken off his saddle. In a moment the winner of the Coventry Stakes was down on his back, squirming and thrashing like a freshly landed trout. And then as the two men stood and watched, enjoying his evident delight, the unthinkable happened. For as Mill Reef burrowed head down in the sand he somehow contrived to slip the bridle over his ears. And in a flash, sensing the unaccustomed freedom, he was up and

away – one of the most valuable two-year-old colts in the
world loose in a paddock with two fillies and five horrified
powerless men.

The gate which could so easily have been left open was
mercifully closed and, galloping up to it, Mill Reef stopped
for a moment, gazing towards the Downs. 'There was nothing
to do but pray,' Ian Balding recalls and the next moment
his prayers were miraculously answered. Ninety-nine horses
out of a hundred, full of corn and loose for the first time
in many months would at the very least have galloped flat
out round the paddock with incalculable results. But Mill
Reef proved to be the hundredth. Turning away from the
gate he trotted back towards his trainer, ignored the snorting
prancing fillies and calmly began to crop grass beside them.
Scarcely daring to breath John Hallum walked up and
slipped the bridle quietly over his head. The whole incident
had lasted less than three minutes.

Its only permanent result – apart perhaps from shortening
the lives of those involved – was that Mill Reef was in future
only allowed to roll in a special sand pit laid for his benefit
inside the covered ride. But he never forgot those moments
of freedom and, at the end of each roll would leap up without warning just on the off-chance of catching John Hallum
unawares. He never in fact got loose again and in all his
life so far as I know, nobody fell off him. But on at least one
occasion that record was in serious danger.

No one, it seems, had seen fit to warn Geoff Lewis that,
at a particular point on the Downs – where the string always
moved from a walk to a trot – Mill Reef was accustomed to
whip round violently. 'I was treading air twice that morning,'
says Geoff. 'It was only the thought of all those ten per
cents that got me back.' And Ian Balding remembers that
his jockey was rendered completely speechless for a full two
minutes – almost certainly a record in its own right.

Like most celebrities, famous horses have to put up with
visitors of various kinds and Mill Reef as a rule treated them

impeccably. But you can have too much of anything and once, as a specially choosy photographer posed him for the hundredth time, the second lot came into view on their way back from the gallops. A senior stableman called Jim Beasant had been detailed for the chore of holding Mill Reef that morning and next moment poor Jim found himself being towed across the paddock on his stomach. His conduct in the next few seconds won no actual medal but it earns him an honourable place in this story. No one could possibly have blamed him for letting go, and to hold on was both difficult, painful and dangerous. But hold on he did and Mill Reef came gradually to a halt. Like all his other misdemeanours this was the product of high spirits not vice and, as I have said, apart from an occasional sharp nip when bored beyond endurance, he never intentionally harmed either a human being or another horse.

Nor did his stable companions ever harm him, but there was one morning on which Morris Dancer of all horses came within an ace of knocking the pride of the yard for six.

Winter in a flat race stable is a time of rest, recuperation and, for both men and horses, considerable boredom. From the start of November at Kingsclere a gradual letting-down process begins with less corn, less work and, from a human point of view at least, much less interest and excitement. No more cantering is done and the string just walks and trots around the paddocks and pathways – or on bad mornings in the covered ride. The fillies and geldings are sent home or turned out to grass but for the colts the worst time is yet to come. It is, ironically Christmas, two days before which they are given a physic or purgative. This not only clears their system but in most cases makes them feel so thoroughly miserable that on Christmas Day they are quite content to stand idle in their boxes while the human race enjoys itself. 'On Boxing Day,' Ian says, 'all of us have hangovers – but at least getting ours was fun.'

A week later the horses are wormed and a week after that

they have their annual Fluvac inoculation. It is in fact a thoroughly uncomfortable period and even Mill Reef at the height of his fame did not escape it. Then after one more week of comparative idleness the build-up begins again and at Kingsclere this means road work, three or four miles to begin with increasing steadily to six or seven by the beginning of March. By no means all flat race trainers are prepared to risk their horses even on quiet country roads and when Ian Balding first took over some of the older lads were heard to grumble 'he must think he's training bloody jumpers'. But Ian stuck to his guns and has, touch wood, had no reason to regret it.

In Mill Reef's second and third winter at Kingsclere the routine was always the same. Royal Rebel, an old and reliable gelding would walk a hundred yards ahead of the string to act as a warning 'buffer' against oncoming traffic. Morris Dancer came next and then Mill Reef, dancing lightly along in knee boots, rugs and hood, enjoying every moment of his morning constitutional, ears cocked enquiringly to the sights and sounds of the village of Ecchinswell through which they passed.

At the end of this six week period – when the string starts cantering again – there comes a particularly anxious time for the trainer. And it was then that the Morris Dancer contretemps occurred.

On the morning of their first canter each season the horses have a specially long trot to get their backs well down and then set off in pairs along a steep uphill three furlong canter. Back on an almost full scale diet, muscled up from the road work and generally raring to go, they are a sight to gladden a trainer's heart – but also one calculated to make him hold his breath for fear of premature explosions.

In March, 1971 the three-year-old Mill Reef had no way of knowing the significance of this particular morning and set off quietly enough in front through a narrow gap at the start of the canter. But Morris Dancer, in his ninth season

at Kingsclere, knew only too well what was up and no doubt
said to his companion, 'come on, let's show these children
how to go'. Well before they were due to set off the two
older horses were totally out of control, storming flat out
through the gap and overtaking the leaders at a perilous rate
of knots. 'It was touch and go,' John Hallum says. 'Old
Morris came past us so close I could feel the wind.' To the
horrified Ian watching from his hack it looked even closer
than that but all, by a whisker, was well. Only one other
horse ever galloped past Mill Reef again.

Though sometimes relaxed to the point of laziness towards
the end of his career he always loved the early morning
gallops high on the downs above Kingsclere – and could pull
like a train when he felt like it. The hardest job of all,
however, was to get him home again.

'He just hated going back to his stable,' says John Hallum,
'used to drag his feet all the way down like a boy going back
to school. If you had let him he would have been a hundred
yards behind the others.' Mill Reef in fact was always easily
bored, particularly by solitude. What he loved was work,
variety and company. It had been a lucky day indeed for
him when the decision was taken which consigned him to
the sweeping downs and tree-lined lanes of Kingsclere instead of the monotonous uniform dirt tracks round which
his compatriots not only race but gallop all their working
lives.

CHAPTER NINE

The Two Thousand Guineas

The customary parades, demonstrations and ceremonies in honour of Karl Marx were no doubt held on May Day 1971, but not at Newmarket. There a bright spring sun turned the great gaunt stands to something like the 'warm yellow' of Paul Mellon's undergraduate memory and the only parades to be seen were long, slow-moving serpentines of cars converging on the Rowley Mile. The magnet which attracted them was the smallest field for a Two Thousand Guineas since 1888 – and one of the most select since, two years before that, Ormonde came from Kingsclere to beat Minting and four others.

Now that racing depends so heavily on betting it is only natural that those responsible for sharing out the Levy Board's largesse should want big fields and 'good open betting races'. But the fact remains that Englishmen still dearly love to see good horses – and will pay to watch them when they meet.

The six who made up the field for the 1971 Two Thousand Guineas had, between them run thirty-three times and won twenty-seven races. With the possible exception of Arkle's second meeting with Mill House no horserace in my memory has excited greater interest or caused more violent differences of opinion. And, as in Ormonde's year (when Fred Archer rode the third favourite Saraband) this was universally regarded as a problem with only three possible solutions.

At the end of 1970 the Jockey Club handicapper Dan

Sheppard had inevitably placed My Swallow and Mill Reef at the top of his Free handicap, with a pound between them to represent the few inches by which My Swallow won the Robert Papin. He had no such obvious yardstick by which to measure Brigadier Gerard but no one could quarrel much with his guess : a single pound behind Mill Reef.

Of the other three runners in the Guineas Minsky had been rated four pounds clear at the top of the Irish Free Handicap, Good Bond, winner of the Horris Hill Stakes, stood nine pounds below My Swallow and Indian Ruler, who had run only once in 1970, did not get a rating.

Good Bond and Indian Ruler had been the first to appear in England as three-year-olds and, winning the Ascot Trial decisively, Good Bond came off nearly seven lengths the better. His trainer Ryan Price was winning races by the hatful in the weeks leading up to the Guineas and, never shy of the odd superlative where his own horses are concerned, had been telling all and sundry that Good Bond was one of the most improved horses in his experience. He was also quoted (by Richard Baerlein) as rating the colt 'two stone in front of Super Honey'. So when Super Honey ran Altesse Royale to one and a half lengths in the One Thousand Guineas all but the most cynical pundits pricked up their ears.

In Ireland meanwhile Minsky had gained two most un-Nijinsky-like victories, scrambling home in each case by a short head. But it was hoped that, like his sire Northern Dancer, he might run better in blinkers and these were to be fitted for the first time in public at Newmarket.

My Swallow's re-appearance, in the Usher Stakes, as the Kempton Trial had been renamed, was both awe-inspiring and inconclusive. Always a colt of tremendous power he had grown and thickened through the winter and, tugging Frankie Durr's arms out from start to finish, gave the impression of a kindly grown-up playing with some rather unathletic children. The opposition was too weak to prove anything new but, when you have My Swallow's record, his

57

admirers were perfectly entitled to ask, who needs anything new?

A week later, anyway, the burden of proof was shifted squarely to Mill Reef. And, maintaining the pressure, as a good cross-examiner should, My Swallow's trainer Paul Davey sent the Doncaster Champagne winner Breeder's Dream to take him on at Newbury in the Greenham Stakes. Two days before that race Mill Reef had galloped clean away from National Park over four-and-a-half furlongs – something he was by no means always able to do. Nevertheless, making the short drive to Newbury on 17 April, Ian Balding could still not altogether put out of his mind the knowledge that Mill Reef's sire Never Bend, himself a superlative two-year-old, had so far produced very few colts half as good in their second season as they had been in their first. By that evening all such unworthy doubts and fears had been set well and truly at rest.

Mill Reef fairly skittled the Greenham field. The critical Newbury audience, though noting that he had grown hardly at all from two to three, could find no other fault with his appearance – and even less with his behaviour in the race. In front from the start he pulled remorselessly away and, beaten four effortless lengths in the end, Breeder's Dream can have taken no very heartening information back to Newmarket. We know now of course that Swing Easy did not truly stay seven furlongs. But he had finished three-and-a-half lengths behind My Swallow over that distance as a two-year-old and Brigadier Gerard had beaten him by an identical margin in the Middle Park. So his running in the Greenham – a long seven lengths behind Mill Reef – looked at the time encouraging to say the least.

There was on the other hand only one-hundredth of a second between My Swallow's time at Kempton and Mill Reef's at Newbury, so neither camp could get much mileage out of that. And while their cards were on the table Brigadier Gerard's were still held firmly against his chest.

After the end of his two-year-old career the Brigadier's owners John and Jean Hislop and his trainer Dick Hern had taken two supremely bold decisions. The first and bravest was for the Hislops, also in a sense the easiest because their brilliant colt had never been for sale. Nevertheless a bid of £250,000 takes some refusing at the best of times, and when they turned it down there seemed every likelihood that Brigadier Gerard might become a very good three-year-old indeed and *still* only finish third in the Two Thousand Guineas. Had he done so his value could scarcely have been as much as £100,000, so let it never be forgotten that his owner's refusal was tantamount to betting at least £150,000 at even money on a horse who, throughout the winter, could be backed for the Two Thousand Guineas at seven or eight to one! I never heard a much better example of judgement laid squarely and bravely on the line.

The second decision – not to give the Brigadier a run in public before the most vital test of his life – was based partly on a belief that he ran best when fresh and partly on John Hislop's conviction that a horse who is wound up too early in the season may be finished before it is half over. But it was a decision that could only have been taken by owners who had total confidence in their trainer, and by a trainer with equal confidence in himself. Even so these two decisions must, together, have made the weeks and days and hours before the Guineas a prolonged and rarefied form of mental torture for Dick Hern.

For the details of Brigadier Gerard's preparation you must look elsewhere – and where better than in his owner's own book? But one gallop should be mentioned here because in it, owing to heavy rain which greatly increased the weight of Joe Mercer's clothes, the Brigadier was asked to meet a four-year-old called Duration on extremely unfavourable terms. So when, just thirty-five minutes before the Two Thousand Guineas was due to start, Duration trotted up in an Apprentice Race on the Rowley Mile – with National

Park in third place eight lengths behind him – it must for the Hislops and Dick Hern have felt like a powerful shot of Benzedrine after a long sleepless night. Had they seen Ian Balding's gallop sheet which recorded that in his final work with National Park Mill Reef had been 'just best' they would no doubt have felt ever better.

Ian in fact was not unduly discouraged, because National Park has always been a great deal better at home than on the racecourse. But by this time he had other things to worry about. At twelve o'clock that morning, visiting Mill Reef in the Links Stables just off the Rowley mile both he and Paul Mellon, over from America for the race, had been delighted. 'That horse looks *ready*,' said his owner – and from an American 'ready' is a very special compliment.

But two hours later, walking out to saddle Mill Reef, Ian was both surprised and dismayed to find the colt in an un-characteristically evil temper. 'He was really ratty to saddle that day,' the trainer recalls; 'he would have eaten you for twopence.' And, to Geoff Lewis entering the paddock, the line of Mill Reef's stomach sloped up ominously steep to-wards his stifle – 'like the Papin all over again'.

It was not, to my eyes, nearly as bad as that, but in fact, as Mill Reef unboxed after the short journey down from the Links, the first horse he saw had been Minsky – cavorting about in a manner which, had a film censor been present, would have earned an immediate X-certificate. Mill Reef, though no prude, was understandably startled and, as at Kempton before the Imperial Stakes came dangerously close to getting away from John Hallum altogether. 'He goes as fast backwards as he does forwards,' John says, 'and a couple of times that day he was very nearly gone.'

All was well in the end, however, and, although he was predictably dwarfed in the paddock by My Swallow and Brigadier Gerard, neither Mill Reef's behaviour nor his appearance – least of all his action cantering to the post – disheartened his supporters. We made him favourite at 6–4 with My Swallow, who looked if anything better than ever, at 2–1 and Brigadier Gerard at 11–2.

In a six horse race the draw should in theory have little or no significance but now Mill Reef (drawn 1) and My Swallow (drawn 6) had the other four between them. And, as My Swallow set off in front, Geoff Lewis took Mill Reef across to join him after only just over a furlong. Supremely confident of his own mount's stamina and courage, he reasoned that the longer and closer fought the battle the more certain Mill Reef was to win it. And win *that* battle he did – so to criticise Geoff is only hindsight.

All the same, just arguably, he was wrong. Mill Reef has never minded racing on his own, and, drawn on the rail he could have come straight home instead of wasting four horses' width to join his rival. Had he done so (this is the hindsight part) Joe Mercer on Brigadier Gerard would have had to choose which of his two opponents to track.

The most common misconception about the 1971 Two Thousand Guineas is that Mill Reef and My Swallow 'cut each others' throats'. Nothing, as the clock confirms, could be further from the truth. In fact, as all the jockeys who took part agree, they went a perfectly normal gallop to half way and had only just begun to race in earnest at the Bushes, when Joe Mercer on Brigadier Gerard was the first to pick up his whip. At that moment, though not exactly confident, Geoff Lewis was perfectly happy in his work, still sure, and rightly so, that Mill Reef would wear My Swallow down when they reached the final hill. But then his left ear picked up an ominous threatening sound.

There has never, in my memory, been a better, more stylish or more rhythmic rider of a flat race finish than Joe Mercer. And, as he starts to ride flat out he hisses in time between his teeth like a boxer punching the heavy bag. It was this hiss-hiss that Geoff heard now, and a second later, as Brigadier Gerard's head came into view he must have known in his heart that the game was up. For that one back-hand slap had acted on the Brigadier like a trumpet call to his namesake's regiment of Hussars. Sweeping down into the dip he produced a burst of speed as dramatic as any seen in a Newmarket classic since the war; from that moment on Mill Reef, though duly avenging his only previous defeat by three-quarters of a length, was beaten fair and square. I said earlier that the 'cut throat' theory was nonsense and surely Brigadier Gerard's time – 1 m. 39.20 s., or just the average for the course – is final proof of that. For if two horses of Mill Reef's and My Swallow's undoubted quality gallop flat out for six furlongs on good going – and are then passed by one of the best milers of all time – it is difficult to believe that the Rowley Mile record would not have been in danger.

But no one who saw this enthralling race could possibly claim that there was the slightest trace of a fluke about Brigadier Gerard's triumph. Certainly no one connected with Mill Reef has ever suggested any such thing. The little horse's nerves beforehand may support the view that he had other, better days. And I agree with Ian Balding that, had Geoff Lewis gone straight home along the rails as fast as ever he was able, the Brigadier might at least have had a rather harder task.

But as Joe Mercer rode back that day – to a rapturous welcome – there was no doubt whatever in the minds of the many experts present that they had seen a great horse at his brilliant best. What few of them realised at the time was that there were two great horses in the 1971 Two Thousand Guineas field. It took several weeks and at least two more races before they accepted that.

CHAPTER TEN

The Derby

Retained in 1971 as Noel Murless's stable jockey (with a special dispensation to ride Mill Reef in all his races), Geoff Lewis had started the three-day Newmarket meeting by choosing Magic Flute in the One Thousand Guineas, only to see her stable mate, Altesse Royale, run out a decisive winner. A painfully narrow defeat followed on Prince Consort in the Jockey Club Stakes and then, just to round it off, two hours after the bitter disappointment of Mill Reef's defeat in the Two Thousand Guineas, a horse called Sequence gave him a crashing fall in the Culford Maiden Stakes.

So Geoff's final memory of a week to which he had been looking forward eagerly all winter was of lying in a hospital bed listening to two doctors discussing whether he had broken his neck or his leg – or both. The answer, happily, was neither, but the impact of the fall had pinched a nerve in his spine and caused partial paralysis of both his hands. Not exactly an ideal state of affairs for a jockey with the Derby just a month away.

As he lay in bed, however, Geoff had one vivid mental picture to console him. It was of the last two hundred yards of the Two Thousand Guineas and of the undiminished power with which Mill Reef had covered them. 'We were really travelling at the death,' he told Ian Balding. 'He'll get the mile and a half for sure.'

Even Ian did not feel quite that confident – and very few

others were confident at all. For several days after the Two Thousand Guineas, in fact, Mill Reef was not even favourite for the Derby, although that race had always been his next target and John Hislop never wavered from his decision not to run Brigadier Gerard at Epsom.

A Le Levanstell colt called Levanter had won the Craven Stakes impressively in April and, with his trainer Ryan Price as optimistic as he had been about Good Bond, it was Levanter who, for a time, headed the ante-post lists. But his spell in the limelight ended abruptly when Linden Tree and Frascati beat him pointless in the Chester Vase. The general picture presented by this and the other traditional classic trials in England, Ireland and France was of a three-year-old generation without a single outstanding member whose ability to stay one and a half miles could be guaranteed. Bourbon, Irish Ball, Millenium and Zug all had their admirers in France and Lombardo, who had beaten the good ex-Italian four-year-old, Ortis, seemed the best from Iceland.

In England, Homeric and Athens Wood finished together in the Lingfield Trial with the handicapper Spoiled Lad between them. L'Apache won at Sandown and Juggernaut scrambled home in a humble Maiden Race at Lingfield. Lester Piggott's choice was as usual the subject of endless bar-room gossip and press-room speculation. But when in the end he opted for The Parson, a big green maiden who had only run three times, the feeling was that even Lester's acknowledged mastery of Epsom might scarcely be adequate this time.

The nearer you got to Epsom, in fact, the more obvious it became that the whole Derby problem was heavily over-shadowed by one question. Would Mill Reef stay a mile and a half? Or rather would he be able, at that distance, to produce the top-class speed which he, alone of all the probable runners, was known for certain to possess?

The case for the prosecution, so to speak, was based mostly on the racing record of Mill Reef's sire, Never Bend. A

The King George VI and Queen Elizabeth Stakes

Drawing away at the close of the Arc de Triomphe

The Prix Ganay: at the Distance

and the winning post – 'ten lengths'!

member of the great Nasrullah's last crop, Never Bend was a brilliant two-year-old – the best of his generation in 1962 – and a winner, at distances from five furlongs to a mile, of what was then a record sum in prize money. Next season, however, though by no means a total wash-out, Never Bend could only finish second in the Kentucky Derby and third in the Preakness Stakes. Kelso beat him easily in the Woodward and his only race over a distance longer than ten furlongs was a dismal failure.

The point often missed, as the breeding pundits pored over this discouraging catalogue, was the vastly different way in which horses are trained and raced in America and Europe. Throughout his career, no attempt was made to settle Never Bend and conserve his stamina – or at least, if made, it was soon abandoned as hopeless. As a two-year-old, almost all his victories were pillar to post affairs and in both the Kentucky Derby and the Preakness, he jumped off in front 'as though the devil was starter'.

It is pointless to speculate now how much or how little Mill Reef would have accomplished if ridden in this way. In fact, from the very beginning, in all his gallops at Kingsclere he was taught to come from behind and, in the strong sympathetic hands of men like John Hallum and Paul Cook (for whom, according to Ian Balding, he went better than anyone at home), he soon acquired the priceless art of relaxation. No doubt a horse's genetic make-up does in the last analysis determine the outer limits of his stamina, but I shall always believe that in many cases those limits can only be realised with the help of top-class horsemen and skilful training.

In any case, Mill Reef's pedigree was by no means exclusively that of a speed merchant. His dam, Milan Mill, had only raced as a two-year-old, but she is by Princequillo and should therefore in theory have stayed at least as well as her half-sister (by Hasty Road), Berkeley Springs who finished second in the Oaks. In general, the Black Ray family has tended to generate a fair amount of stamina, though in May 1971 it had not yet turned out an actual Classic winner.

Mill Reef had come back from Newmarket showing little or no sign of his hard race in the Guineas and now, as the arguments raged about his stamina, he went back to work as though nothing untoward had happened. A fortnight after the Guineas, he galloped five furlongs with Morris Dancer and finished 'hacking'. Four days later, Private Walk led him for a mile and Ian Balding's comment was 'keen but nicely settled'.

The same, however, could hardly be said of Ian himself for, though keen enough, he was far from settled – all too well aware that the eyes of the racing world were fixed, as never before, on his handling of Mill Reef.

Coming, as it does, early in the sixth month of a thorough-bred's third year, the Derby is, in effect, a contest for immature adolescents. So, while all trainers walk a tightrope between too much work and too little, those responsible for Derby colts are in the position of marksmen aiming at one tiny all-important bullseye on a constantly shifting target. Just occasionally, no doubt, that bullseye has been hit by luck and certainly some Derby winners have had so much in hand that they could arguably have won despite their trainer. But a three-year-old colt at this stage of his career is such a delicate mechanism that even one false move is probably one too many. For this reason, it seems to me that the trainer who stands in the winner's circle on Derby Day deserves, in a real sense, to be called a master of his art.

It follows that a young man with his first seriously fancied Derby runner faces a whole new set of problems. And, unless confident to the point of arrogance, he can only examine – and make his own choice from – the methods by which those problems have been solved by others in the past.

Ian Balding's earliest experience with flat race horses had

been as assistant to Herbert Blagrave at Beckhampton and he was inevitably steeped in tales of the great Fred Darling, trainer, like John Porter, of seven Derby winners. As he understood it, all those winners had been worked over the full mile-and-a-half or something very close to it, doing their last serious gallop on the Saturday, only four days before the Derby.

But Ian had also studied an alternative method practised in Tipperary by another acknowledged genius, Vincent O'Brien. Neither Sir Ivor nor Nijinsky was ever worked, before Epsom, over anything like the full Derby distance and both did their last full-scale gallop a week or more before the race. Clearly Mill Reef had far more in common with these two brilliant American-bred horses than with massive animals like Captain Cuttle and Coronach. So, after much heart-searching, Ian decided to adopt the O'Brien method – or rather, to adapt it to his own needs. And that meant resisting the temptation to settle, for his own peace of mind, the question of Mill Reef's stamina.

He planned the most crucial part of his programme ten days before the Derby and so, on the night of 22 May, Geoff Lewis came back to Kingsclere from Newbury races. After a week's convalescence in the South of France, Geoff had resumed at Brighton four days earlier and his first ride back was an effortless victory on Paddy's Progress. Things went well all week and although the strength of his right hand was still only partially restored, there had, I remember, been no trace of weakness visible as he drove home Random Shot to win at Newbury that afternoon.

Next morning, however, Ian's plans encountered one of those little local difficulties with which English trainers learn to live. As the first lot pulled out, a thick fog lay over Kingsclere and when he, Geoff Lewis, Philip Waldron and Paul Cook arrived at the gallop known as 'the left-hand side', you had to strain your eyes to see a horse a hundred yards away. It was the sort of morning on which, a century earlier,

John Porter used to hear Ormonde – who, as a four-year-old, became a roarer – from fully half a mile.

But the Derby waits for no man and so, not without misgivings, Ian launched the three horses into the murk, clicking his stop-watch as he did so. The 'left-hand side' runs downhill for three furlongs from the mile-and-a-quarter pole where they started that morning, then round a sweeping left-hand turn and into a straight of nearly six furlongs, every yard of which is on the collar. The plan was for Aldie to lead for six furlongs or so and then for Bright Beam to take over. Geoff Lewis was to track them until the final uphill quarter-mile and come on – if he could. Both older horses were receiving about a stone, so Mill Reef, who started a few lengths behind, was meeting them on terms roughly thirty-two pounds worse than normal weight-for-age.

From the start of the gallop, Ian had only a quarter of a mile to go to reach the finish and his hack that morning – a favourite point-to-pointer called The Brigand – covered it with time to spare. So much time in fact that, to his rider, peering anxiously through the fog, there seemed an agonising age to wait.

And when, at last, a dim grey shape loomed up – alone – the awful thought flashed through Ian's mind that it was Aldie, who is grey. But only for a moment. Fifty yards off, Geoff Lewis's crouch was unmistakable and, as Mill Reef sailed past with the others still barely visible, Ian snapped his watch again. The time, two minutes twenty-two seconds, would be slow for ten furlongs on a racecourse, but on that gallop and in those conditions, it seemed to the trainer more than satisfactory.

Mill Reef, in fact, had been so relaxed in the early stages of the gallop that Geoff Lewis too had to suffer his moment of doubt.

'I thought, Oh God, he doesn't get it after all,' he remembers. 'But one little tap down the neck was all he needed.'

'I'll go past them so fast they'll catch pneumonia,' Geoff

told Ian as they walked back off the downs and although of course they both knew in their hearts how misleading such gallops can be, breakfast still tasted pretty good that morning.

Talking of breakfast, it may be of interest here to describe Mill Reef's own diet at this crucial stage of his life. His breakfast that morning would have been served – by Bill Palmer – at 5.30 a.m. – two and a half pounds of dry oats, the Canadian ones he ate throughout his active life. Returning from the gallop and having been groomed for at least half an hour by John Hallum, he would get seven more pounds of oats, a double handful of bran and either chaff, cut grass or chopped dandelions, of which he was particularly fond. That had to last him until 6.30 p.m. and the main meal of the day. To ten pounds of oats, the bran and chaff or whatever, as before, there were added six eggs (carefully shelled) and half a pound of honey.

'It looked good enough to eat yourself,' Emma Balding says – and Mill Reef very seldom left a mouthful. If, in fact, he had cleaned up by 10.30, when Bill Palmer took his last look round, a final two pounds of dry oats was always on offer. And that was almost always gone by morning.

For so good a 'doer', Mill Reef was not, oddly enough , a greater eater of hay. Because of a tragic accident with one of the Queen's horses, Ian Balding never risked giving him a hay net and he used to scatter the stuff all over his box, picking only what took his fancy. John Hallum would already have spent hours searching the barn for the choicest, sweetest-smelling morsels, and woe betide anyone caught with their hands on one of his selected bales.

Mill Reef went back to the downs only twice more before Derby Day. Philip Waldron rode him a mile tucked in behind Winter Fair on 26 May and three days later, four days before the race itself, he came five furlongs sharp up the undulating 'Monday morning' gallop.

The zest and fire with which he moved that day gladdened Ian Balding's heart, but nothing could set his mind altogether at rest. The horse had done everything asked of him, but had enough – or perhaps too much – been asked? That is the trainer's eternal dilemma, and the trainer of an Epsom Derby favourite has other worries besides.

Security is one of them and by this time, the block of boxes where Mill Reef lived had already been fitted with burglar alarms. To make assurance doubly sure, an off-duty policeman, complete with a small but pugnacious terrier, kept watch at night and when the horsebox left for Epsom it was preceded by a Securicor van containing two armed guards.

There remained the problem of the uniquely long preliminaries on Derby Day and the obvious danger that by far the biggest crowd Mill Reef had yet encountered might cause him to repeat his Kempton and Newmarket antics. On both those occasions, he had shied left-handed away from John Hallum, so it was now decided that he should have two attendants, one on either side. And with this decision, a new, important and colourful personality enters the story.

Tom Reilly had already been the blacksmith at Kingsclere for more than twenty years, ever since the days of Evan Williams, from whom Peter Hastings-Bass took over the yard. A native of Dunboyne, Co Meath, Tom was one of the first men ever to put a shoe on Golden Miller and had plated many great Irish horses in his time, notably Prince Regent and Hatton's Grace. While on honeymoon in England just after the war, Tom was, he says, 'kidnapped' by Lord Derby's racing secretary and worked for a time at Stanley House, where George Colling was then the trainer.

When, later on, he told Colling that he had a good offer of a job with Evan Williams, the trainer promptly bet him £10 he would not last a year, describing Kingsclere as 'the last place God made on the Earth'.

'Poor Mr Colling,' Tom says. 'He died himself before the year was out, so I never collected my bet. But I never went back, either.'

Quite apart from the obvious desirability of having your own blacksmith on hand, Tom had all the qualities of a perfect bodyguard : great strength, unshakeable calm and a voice which Mill Reef already knew and trusted. So he was an obvious choice for the job and it is a matter of record that, from then on, flanked by his faithful entourage, Mill Reef was never seriously frightened or upset again on any of his journeys.

On those journeys – the part of them spent in the horsebox – the little horse's chief requirement was company and Bill Jennings recalls how, if left for too long to his own devices, he would become bored and restive.

'But then one of us would just go back and talk to him,' Bill says, 'and he would be right as rain.'

So off they went, the four of them, Bill, John Hallum, Tom Reilly and Mill Reef, to keep their date with the world and his wife on Epsom Downs. Considerable pressure had been put on Ian Balding to travel the horse a day earlier so that he could spend the last night in the heavily guarded racecourse stables. But remembering Mill Reef's nervous state before the Guineas the trainer stuck to his guns. The horsebox left early on 2 June, 1971, and that was just as well, for as anyone who went to the Derby that sweltering day remembers all too clearly, the whole Epsom area was one vast traffic jam from midday onwards.

The European Cup Final was being played in London and a large proportion of the Metropolitan Police Force seemed to be attending it. Their place was taken by a motley array of traffic wardens, some of whom scarcely seemed to know the difference between left, right and straight on. One of the traditional fairgrounds had been re-sited on Epsom Downs, the new tunnel under the course between the finish and the paddock caused unexpected complications, and all these factors combined with a glorious sunny day and a huge crowd to produce a high degree of overheated chaos.

Ian Balding, who had Winter Fair to saddle in the race

before the Derby, was among those inextricably bogged down within two miles of the course and had to run for it, top hat and all, leaving Emma and his mother-in-law to do the best they could. By that time Mill Reef had long been secure in the racecourse stables, whiling away the time by tapping his forefeet against the concrete door frame. His own box at Kingsclere had been give a special 'Tartan' surface like an Olympic running track and John Hallum thinks that the different feel and sound of the concrete amused and interested him. However that may be, he managed to knock both front shoes out of place and Tom Reilly had to replate him before he left for the paddock. There, cool, elegant and untroubled by the thronging crowds, he added a badly needed touch of class to what was by common consent a somewhat undistinguished-looking field.

'Until he entered the Parade Ring,' Roger Mortimer wrote, 'one got the impression that the drab uniformity of the classless society had spread to the equine world.'

To those who had not seen him since Newmarket, Mill Reef had clearly put on weight and muscle and although two small patches of sweat appeared on his flanks just before he was saddled, they had vanished before the Parade.

The going at Epsom was as near perfect as makes no difference and, cantering past the stands, Mill Reef would surely have cut any daisies that happened to be growing there. He always gallops with his head and neck well stretched and Geoff Lewis always rode him on a longer than average rein. On Derby Day, I remember noting anxiously that he seemed to be pulling harder than usual, but Geoff thinks this impression was due to the slight remaining weakness in his own hands. And in any case, leaving nothing to chance, Ian Balding had stationed a senior stable-lad called Paddy Heffernan (who had come to Epsom with Winter Fair) down in the paddock just in case Mill Reef should arrive there going too fast. In fact, he pulled up calmly enough and Paddy accompanied him across the road and down the narrow crowd-lined gangway which leads up to the Derby start.

Meanwhile, to the unkind amusement of some and the despair of others, the much-fancied French colt Bourbon had lost both his temper, his bridle and, for a while, his jockey in front of the stands. The blinkers which had galvanised Bourbon in the Prix Hocquart now appeared to madden him and although the Clerk of the Course, Major Peter Beckwith-Smith, was able (to his eternal credit) to conjure up a spare bridle, it still took the combined efforts of Bourbon's trainer, Alec Head, his son Freddy and a co-operative mounted policeman to get the recalcitrant colt back past the stands. By the time he arrived at the start, needless to say, Bourbon's chances had evaporated in a cloud of steam and wasted energy. (Poor Freddy Head cannot have the happiest memories of Epsom, for the following year, Lyphard carried him so wide round Tattenham Corner that, according to an uncharitable rival jockey, 'the gypsies in the fairground were asking for danger money'.) Bourbon's antics, in fact, served one useful purpose because, but for them, Priscilla Hastings and Emma Balding would have missed the Derby. It was only as Mr Alec Marsh got the field away (four minutes late) that they arrived, hot and panting, in the stands. There followed, at least for them and Mill Reef's other supporters, the sort of race that usually happens only in one's dreams.

They went, for the first three sharply uphill furlongs, only a moderate gallop. Linden Tree, blinkered for the first time and pulling hard, was up in front with Credit Man, whose rider, Yves Saint Martin, was, as a matter of interest, to make the early running in three successive Epsom Derby rides.

In those first two furlongs, as the films show, Mill Reef was tossing his head impatiently against the bit and looked, for a moment, like pulling his way undesirably close to the leaders. But Geoff quickly covered him up behind Beaming

73

Lee and Credit Man and, by the top of Tattenham Hill where Linden Tree had gone a length clear in front, the favourite was tucked in sixth or seventh, three horses off the inside rail.

It is here – down the hill to Tattenham Corner – that most hard luck stories are born in the Derby. About half the runners are already either beaten or at full strentch and, to a jockey coming from behind, they represent a field of floating mines in which his chances can all too easily be blown sky high.

Now, halfway down the hill, Geoff Lewis had one such hazard to negotiate. He had always hoped to track Joe Mercer and Homeric into the straight, partly because Joe could be relied on better than most to keep his horse balanced and partly because, on his Lingfield form, Homeric seemed reasonably sure to be somewhere near the leaders. Both assumptions proved correct but now, with Homeric outside him and half a length ahead, Geoff saw Credit Man begin to falter and fall back slap in Mill Reef's path.

A picture taken only seconds later at Tattenham Corner shows how completely the Irish colt collapsed, for in it he has only three behind him. That is what I mean by floating mines and, to avoid this one, Geoff desperately needed a yard or so of elbow-room. Joe Mercer had every right, in theory, to deny him and could have done so without the slightest danger to himself or Homeric. There are some jockeys of whom, as Geoff says, 'You'd as soon call for room as ask Scrooge for a quid,' but Joe Mercer is not one of them. Now, hearing Geoff's urgent shout, he edged Homeric out a fraction and, with Credit Man hanging the other way, a providential gap appeared.

To take it, however, Mill Reef had to quicken sharply and the next few seconds confirmed the truth that an ideal Derby colt needs many of the characteristics of a top class polo pony. For, having darted outside Credit Man, Geoff was able to ease back in again behind Homeric in half a dozen strides. Seen on film, it is a memorable display of handiness and, as a result of it, swinging down into Tattenham Corner, Mill Reef was poised ideally in fourth place with only Linden Tree, Lombardo and Homeric between him and the winning post.

There were, of course, more than three furlongs still to go, but in the twenty-odd Derbys I have watched, I do not remember one in which the result was more predictable so far from home. Linden Tree was still going strong and so for another furlong was Lombardo. But every line of Geoff Lewis's body shouted confidence and with all his three rivals at full stretch, Mill Reef was cruising on the bit.

He did not win like that, though, and, to the very short list of horses who ever fully extended him, the gallant Linden Tree's name must now be added. For a moment, two furlongs out, Linden Tree himself looked sure to be passed by Lombardo and he had only just repelled that challenge, when Mill Reef sailed up the middle of the course to join him. To us in the stands it looked all over, but Duncan Keith did not think so, nor did Linden Tree. With nearly a furlong left, Geoff had to pull his whip through on Mill Reef and ring urgently for full speed ahead. The response was immediate and decisive but Geoff did not stop riding and the two lengths by which he won could not, I think, have been very much increased. Poor Linden Tree : this desperate struggle was, as it turned out, his final bow, for three weeks later in the Irish Derby, he refused to race at all. But on 2 June, 1971 he was a very good three-year-old indeed, good enough, one might guess, to win at least six Derbys out of ten.

Behind him now, Lombardo clearly failed to stay, Homeric could not quicken and, past them both came Irish Ball, the only horse in the race who could in any sense of the word be called 'unlucky'.

Irish Ball's chief misfortune was that Lester Piggott, who could have ridden him, chose The Parson instead. For having, by his own account, got into all sorts of trouble down the hill, the French jockey A. Gibert proceeded up the straight to give a lifelike imitation of an over-excited wind-mill. His antics sent poor Irish Ball rolling first this way then that and in the end, it was an heroic achievement on the horse's part to finish third. On the Curragh, a course much better suited to M. Gibert's methods, Irish Ball was later to slam Lombardo and he also ran a courageous second in the Washington D.C. International to Mill Reef's childhood friend, Run The Gantlet.

Geoff Lewis had one more moment of anxiety on Derby Day, for Linden Tree (and who shall blame him?) threatened to lash out as Mill Reef passed behind him after pulling up. The broadest, happiest grin on Epsom Downs vanished for an instant from Geoff's face, but all was well.

So back they came in triumph – greeted first by a speech-less John Hallum, then by Bill Jennings and Paddy Heffernan and, a close fourth by Dai Davies, the cheerful, tireless Welshman whose exhausting job it is to relay via the Press Association the news of great events like this as near as possible before they happen. To Dai, Paul Mellon described it as 'the happiest day of my life', and John Hallum felt the same. Of all the great memories Mill Reef left him, this comes first.

'To do a Derby winner' – he says – 'No lad can ever ask for more than that.'

That evening, when Mill Reef's horsebox got back to Kingsclere, the village was *en fête*. Flags and bunting hung across the road and a happy crowd had gathered at the turning off towards Park House. 'They wanted us to get him out there,' John Hallum recalls, 'and when we wouldn't they ran behind us all the way home.'

At last Mill Reef unboxed in triumph and, for half an hour, walked graciously among his fans in front of a row of cottages which have since been named after him. It had been a long hard day but if he was tired it did not show. Patted and stroked from head to tail, he remained as calm and unflustered as he and Geoff Lewis had been throughout the Derby.

As Ian Balding stood watching him, his thoughts went back to the time, seven years before when he had pondered so long and anxiously whether to take over at Kingsclere. It had meant giving up a life he loved but that happy summer evening, with the roar of the Epsom crowd still ringing in his ears, all the worry and trouble seemed infinitely well worthwhile.

CHAPTER ELEVEN

Glorious Summer

Of all the tired clichés that fill the air in racecourse bars and the columns on racing pages the question 'Yes, but what did he beat?' is heard as often as any. It is asked after almost every Derby and no three-year-old, however outstanding among his contemporaries, can answer it conclusively until he has met and conquered older horses.

So in 1971, although Irish Ball and Lombardo confirmed the Epsom form by finishing first and second in the Irish Derby, there were still those who, pointing to Mill Reef's defeat in the Two Thousand Guineas, argued that he might be no more than the best in an ordinary crop of middle distance three-year-olds. The memory of Nijinsky was still fresh in many minds and in the weeks that followed Epsom anyone suggesting that it might shortly be overshadowed would have been regarded as an optimistic dreamer.

Mill Reef's next target had always been the Eclipse Stakes and as the day of that race approached it became clear that the opposition would include at least two yardsticks by which his merit could indeed be accurately measured.

Two years earlier Mr Jim Joel's Welsh Pageant had finished third in the Two Thousand Guineas. But in 1970, beaten only once, he established himself as one of the best, most consistent milers in Europe and two months before the Eclipse he had confirmed that status as a five-year-old by winning the Lockinge Stakes. At Sandown admittedly Welsh Pageant would be attempting a distance beyond a mile for the first time but on his favourite dry fast going there was no obvious reason why he should not stay. With Lester Piggott on his back he was in fact by any reckoning a formidable rival for a three-year-old.

But not as it turned out the most formidable rival that Mill Reef had to face. For by July that year the form book stated unequivocally that Countess Margit Batthyanny's Caro was the outstanding ten furlong horse in Europe. Close to the top class as a three-year-old (he won the French Two Thousand Guineas on a disqualification and finished third to Sassafras in the French Derby) Caro had swept the board in France in the spring and early summer of 1971. In the Prix d'Harcourt, the Prix Ganay and the Prix Dollar he gave three ruthlessly efficient displays, always assisted by a pace-maker and always producing at the finish a turn of foot to which his rivals (who included horses like Miss Dan, Stintino, Faraway Son, Gold Rod and Dictus) could find no effective answer.

In twenty-four runnings at Sandown since the war only seven three-year-olds had won the Eclipse by 1971 and while there are various possible explanations for that statistic the twelve pound weight-for-age allowance in early July certainly does not give the younger generation any noticeable advantage. At least arguably the reverse is true and if, as some critics still maintain, Mill Reef was just an 'ordinary' Derby winner then without much doubt either Welsh Pagent or Caro or both would surely be good enough to reveal his limitations.

For Geoff Lewis Mill Reef's Derby had been only the beginning of a singularly triumphant week. No one had ever before won the Derby, Oaks, and Coronation Cup in the same year and Geoff's victories on Mill Reef, Altesse Royale and Lupe had killed stone dead the old canard that he was not a 'big race' jockey.

The two horses chiefly responsible for that unfair and insulting generalisation had been Silly Season and Park Top – both brilliant on their day but both extremely difficult rides whose talents could only be exploited to the full by split second timing and abnormal confidence. Silly Season, at least in his third and final year, became a real jockey's nightmare, a desperately hard puller who downed tools at once if allowed to strike the front a yard too soon. For Ian Balding and Geoff Lewis he came to Kingsclere at the worst possible moment, just as Ian took over the stable. Peter Hastings-Bass had for years been taking special pains to bolster his stable jockey's confidence. 'Sit and suffer,' he used to say. 'The openings will come and even if they don't there is always another day.' With the best will in the world Ian Balding, struggling to prove himself, could hardly be expected to take so relaxed a view, particularly about the best horse in his yard and, as a result Geoff Lewis used to go out on Silly Season with a heavy load of care depressing his normal exuberance. The 1966 Eclipse was only one of several frustrating experiences the horse gave him that year for although Silly Season would probably not have won it in any case he got into a dreadful tangle halfway up the straight and should have finished a good deal closer.

The Duke of Devonshire's lovely and courageous mare Park Top was both a better racehorse and an easier ride than Silly Season but, like him, she did best when ridden from behind and tended to think the race was over once she took the lead. After storming clear in the Cumberland Lodge Stakes at Ascot as a four-year-old, for instance, she was astonishingly caught and beaten by Chicago. It was with that painful memory in mind that Geoff set out to ride her in the 1969 Eclipse.

Determined not to make the same mistake again he refused a tempting opening on the rails two furlongs out and then, as Lester Piggott shot through it on Wolver Hallow, was forced to pull the mare laboriously wide before beginning her run from an impossible position. Few jockeys in my memory have been more universally and comprehensively criticised after an important race and, however unfair he felt

A champion in action: at the finish of the Ganay

Close victory from Homeric in the Coronation Cup

Two studies of Mill Reef and Miss
Claire Balding

some of that criticism to be Geoff would not have been human if so traumatic a failure had not left its mark. To him therefore despite his triple triumph at Epsom the 1971 Eclipse was very much more than just another valuable race. For both horse and man in fact it was in the fullest sense a moment of truth.

I was covering the 1971 Eclipse for ITV and, from the overheated commentator's greenhouse perched above the Sandown Paddock Caro's powerful frame and bright grey coat were an ominously impressive sight. But then Mill Reef walked in and at once my mind went back to Royal Ascot twelve months earlier. Then, as I have said, he had come as close to my ideal of physical perfection as any horse before or since, and now, with quarters as round and shiny as a newly peeled horse-chestnut, he was back at that same peak of health and symmetry. Since Derby Day he had put on weight and muscle in all the important places and, though still small beside his older rivals he looked so beautiful, balanced and deadly that it was for them, not him, that you felt afraid.

Mill Reef and Caro both had pacemakers and Ian Balding anxiously enquired of Tommy Carter beforehand how fast he intended to go on Bright Beam. 'Don't you worry,' Tommy replied. 'I'll know when the times comes.'

He did too but in fact flat out was only barely fast enough because Welsh Pageant, a confirmed front runner, exploded so violently from the stalls that it took Bright Beam more than a furlong to catch him. As for Caro's 'assistant' Quebracho, he was never able to play his intended part at all.

As Bright Beam scorched down the Railway straight Geoff Lewis settled Mill Reef in fourth place with only Caro and the top class handicapper Quayside left behind him. But with Mill Reef there were none of Park Top's foibles to worry about and, turning uphill for home Geoff allowed the little horse to stride gaily past his exhausted stable companion. Both Caro and Quayside followed Mill Reef through outside the leaders and now, ironically, Lester Piggott (whose brilliant opportunism had won the race for Wolver Hollow two years earlier) fell into much the same trap which had ensnared Park Top. Caught in a pocket on the rails with one tired horse (Bright Beam) in front and another (Quebracho) on his left Welsh Pagent was swept back like flotsam on a broken wave from second place to last. It made no difference to the result but by the time he struggled round behind Quebracho the race had reached and passed its climax.

Nor will that climax easily be forgotten by anyone who saw it. For now as Mill Reef struck the front with two and a half furlongs left, Caro who had been poised at his quarters, quickened smoothly to draw level. There he stayed for fifty yards or so and, for that distance far more than a £25,000 first prize hung in the balance.

The end, when it came, was not at first spectacular because no horse travelling as fast as these two were can possibly produce a sudden or explosive burst of speed. But two furlongs out as Mill Reef's admirers held their breath Maurice Philipperon picked up his whip, as he did so the familiar sheepskin noseband showed in front. There was no question of surrender or collapse but in every single one of the three hundred yards remaining poor Caro was left further and further behind. Mill Reef won in the end by four lengths and as usual seemed to be galloping even stronger past the post than at any other stage. His time, 2 m. 5.50 s., set a new course record.

Lester Piggott, third in the end on Welsh Pageant felt that he might have finished second with a clearer run but neither he nor anyone else questioned the utter decisiveness of Mill Reef's victory. Caro's enormously experienced trainer Albert Klimscha summed up the general feeling when he said, 'It is no disgrace to be beaten by a great horse and this *is* a great one – greater than Nijinsky.' It was I think the first occasion on which that overworked adjective had been seriously used to describe Mill Reef, at least as a three-year-old, and although he had not then equalled Nijinsky's achievements few if any of those who saw the 1971 Eclipse were prepared to dispute M Klimscha's statement.

There remained, however, one more possible area of doubt. The Eclipse is a mile-and-a-quarter race and, recalling the slow early gallop in the Derby, it was still conceivable that Mill Reef might be a mile-and-a-quarter horse who had only won at Epsom because his stamina was not sufficiently tested. That, anyway, was the reasoning on which several trainers and jockeys laid their plans for his next race, the King George VI and Queen Elizabeth Stakes, run at Ascot three weeks after the Eclipse.

Peter Walwyn, for instance, decided that the best hope for his Italian Derby winner Ortis (who a month earlier had won the Hardwicke Stakes over the same course and distance by no less than eight lengths) lay in a flat out gallop from start to finish. He ran Loud to ensure just that and so faithfully did Ortis's pacemaker perform his duties that Tommy Carter and Bright Beam were content for once to play second fiddle. When after six furlongs Loud had shot his bolt, Lester Piggott sent Politico past him, doubtless with the same tactical object in mind. But to us in the stands it was already clear by that time that his and Peter Walwyn's planning was based on a false premise.

For Mill Reef, cruising up into third place on the turn for home was ready now to settle once and for all any lingering doubts about his stamina. Geoff Lewis, who in any case had never shared them, called for his effort early in the straight and Ortis who had just taken over from Politico was tossed aside like a leaf in an autumn gale.

Unlike some of his contempories, Lester Piggott for instance, Geoff Lewis has never cared much for motionless 'cat and mouse' victories. So now he kept Mill Reef going with hands and heels until the last fifty yards and, as a result, was quite unable to pull him up until fully two furlongs past the post! Six lengths back Ortis stayed on well to take second place, Acclimatisation was third another three lengths away and Stintino (third in Nijinsky's Derby the year before) was fourth. The others including Irish Ball (who ran unaccountably badly) Politico (third in Nijinsky's St Leger) Guillemot (third in the 1971 Irish Derby) and Nor (fourth to Nijinsky at the Curragh) were so far behind that they looked like creatures of a different, lesser breed.

In the twenty years since Supreme Court went out from Kingsclere to capture the first King George VI and Queen Elizabeth Stakes no horse had ever won it by as much as six lengths. And as in most of his major triumphs Mill Reef's winning margin was expanding rapidly with every yard he travelled. It was at Ascot in fact that I first noticed (though on film it is equally apparent at Sandown) one of his most remarkable characteristics. Almost all horses, even great ones, start to ease up when their rider drops his hands. But Mill Reef at his best did exactly the opposite. He seemed to revel in showing the full extent of his superiority and, once in top gear, needed little if any encouragement.

Of all the distinguished experts present at Ascot in July 1971 none, I suppose, had wider or more intimate experience of top class horses than Lester Piggott. And he, who misses so little worth noticing in a race, summed up Mill Reef with typical economy of words. 'He just keeps going,' Lester said with a sort of wonder in his voice, and added, to Geoff Lewis, a view he has since confirmed to me, namely that Mill Reef was as good that day as any horse he ever saw.

To Geoff Lewis himself the King George, despite what came after it, remains Mill Reef's most memorable performance. 'Daylight was second at Ascot,' he says. 'If I'd given him one slap the judge would have left his box before the others got there.'

One more comment is worth quoting and it came from Monsieur Jean Romanet the charming, infinitely hardworking Frenchman who, as Secretary of the Societé d'Encouragement, he has done more than any other man to guide, inspire and regulate the meteoric rise of his country's racing industry since the war. When someone asked M. Romanet at Ascot whether Mill Reef might now be good enough for the Prix d'Arc d'Triomphe his answer was brief and to the point. 'I wonder,' he said, 'if the Arc is good enough for him.'

CHAPTER TWELVE

Arc de Triomphe

'*Doucement*,' said Tom Reilly '*doucement*, you son of a bachelor.' It was just about the only word of French Tom knew and, as the big grey horsebox roared through the outskirts of Paris on the morning of 3 October, 1971 he was using it, on Ian Balding's instructions, in the hope of toning down the driver's natural Gallic exuberance. 'I said it so often the fellow was looking at me very odd before we got there,' Tom remembers, and to Ian, following anxiously in a hired car, the horsebox's progress did not look nearly *douce* enough. But it arrived safely all the same and as Mill Reef disembarked in the bustling sunlit stable-yard at Longchamp the last leg of his most important journey was over.

The journey in question had been minutely planned long in advance like a major military operation and, like a previous invasion of France, its success depended on a high degree of Anglo-American co-operation. Remembering Mill Reef's first nightmare trip across the channel Ian had suggested to Mr Mellon that they should approach the United States Air Force for the use of their base at Greenham, less than ten minutes down the road from Kingsclere. The permission took a long time to arrive and when, at last it was granted the officer responsible showed Ian a file of correspondence weighing at least ten pounds.

'Don't ever ask me to go through that again,' he said and apparently the question of Mill Reef's right to VIP treat-

86

ment had caused a major flutter in the highest dovecots of
the Air Ministry and the Pentagon.

To laymen no doubt it seemed a lot of trouble to take
about a mere animal and a certain Sergeant Hinz, amazed
by all the fuss, asked Ian what made this horse so 'all fired
special'. Ian replied that Mill Reef had recently been insured
(for this one journey only) for two million pounds. The
Sergeant was suitably impressed. 'Why, Goddammit, he's
worth more than any of my aeroplanes,' he muttered, and
went off at once to check the runway for non-existent pot-
holes.

Having once given their consent, the American Air Force
entered wholeheartedly into the spirit of the enterprise and
as a result, on the morning of Thursday, 39 September, Mill
Reef and Aldie were airborne in a special Boeing Jet (the
same one Nijinsky had used the year before) barely half an
hour after leaving their own boxes. There had, it is true, been
one awkward moment when John Hallum's and Bill
Jennings's passports were found to be still at Kingsclere but
some fast driving by Ian's Secretary Jack Bainton put that
right without delaying the operation.

The object of all this careful planning was of course the
Prix de l'Arc de Triomphe, and since no horse trained in
England had managed to win Europe's richest race since
Migoli twenty-three years earlier Ian understandably felt that
as little as possible should be left to chance. He was also
well aware that his skill as a trainer was on trial as never
before – even more in a way than during the weeks leading
up to the Derby.

The King George VI and Queen Elizabeth Stakes had been
Mill Reef's fifth important race of the season and when he
won it he had been in hard training without a break since
March. For a month after Ascot, therefore, Ian gave him a
complete mental and physical rest. At such a time Kingsclere
has many advantages over a crowded public training centre
like Newmarket or Lambourn. There is such a variety of quiet

lanes and pathways that Mill Reef never had to take the same route two days running and hardly saw another horse. When he did canter it was on one of the winter gallops near the stables – well away from the downs associated in his mind with serious work. But while letting a horse down in this way is easy enough, bringing him back to his peak again as late in the year as October is quite another matter.

One advantage of Mill Reef's defeat in the Two Thousand Guineas had been that it removed any temptation to chase that mythical and, in the writer's opinion, much over-rated chimera, the 'Triple Crown'. No one who watched him at the finish of the King George VI can seriously doubt that Mill Reef would have got the trip well enough to win a St Leger, but Ian was convinced that Nijinsky's exertions over a distance beyond his best had at least contributed to his defeat in the Arc, and neither he nor Mr Mellon ever seriously contemplated submitting Mill Reef to that double ordeal.

At the beginning of September therefore Mill Reef went back to the gallops and on the 11th his owner (mounted on Aldie's half-brother Macaroon, an animal of funereal tendencies known to one and all as 'Mack the Hack') watched him work a mile and three furlongs with Winter Fair. It was the longest, stiffest gallop he ever did as a three-year-old and Ian Balding is inclined now to regret it. For although Mill Reef strode out pretty well that morning, not long afterwards a note of uneasiness begins to creep into Ian's comments on his gallops. On 19 September, a Sunday morning, Mill Reef, Aldie and National Park went to Newbury racecourse and, on fast going, covered a mile and a quarter in a time, hand-clocked, within half a second of the course record. But even so Mill Reef finished only a length and a half in front and although he put a brave face on things for the benefit of the attendant press Ian was not completely happy. Four days later, ridden by Geoff Lewis, the little horse was only 'just best' in a mile work-out with Aldie and on 28

September, two days before leaving for France, he 'lacked sparkle' against that well known morning glory National Park.

Remembering how Mill Reef had fretted and starved himself at Maisons Laffitte Ian took him to spend a night at Salisbury two weeks before the Arc. The little horse settled down well in the quiet empty stables and Ian got permission from the French Authorities to use their special 'Visitors' yard at Lamorlaye. Called 'La Camargo' it is an oasis of calm, far from the noise and hectic activity of Longchamp and here, less than four hours after leaving the yard at Kingsclere, Mill Reef and Aldie were safely installed on Thursday, 30 September. John Hallum, Bill Jennings and Tom Reilly slept in rooms above them and their only companions in the delightful little yard were Ortis and his entourage.

On Saturday morning Mill Reef did his final gallop with Aldie, who, since no pacemaker was needed in the Arc, had been chosen as the ideal travelling companion. This was the work already described in which Ian first noticed the difference between their hoof prints. Both he and John Hallum were reassured by the zest with which Mill Reef sailed up a special private strip of watered ground kindly put at their disposal by the groundsman. But, all the same neither slept too sound that night.

Paris was already full of eager race-goers from all over the world and next morning, as Mill Reef arrived at Longchamp, London Airport seemed to have been taken over altogether by the Turf. It was a glorious sunny day – a day for quenching your thirst as well as soothing your nerves – and long before the runners for the Arc appeared the little bar by the paddock which has always had a special Anglo-Irish flavour was doing a roaring trade.

The British Ambassador, Sir Christopher Soames, himself an enthusiastic owner, had given a huge and delicious lunch party at the Embassy and through a haze of champagne the thought occurred to me how much two great Englishmen, the Ambassador's father-in-law Sir Winston Churchill and the Duke of Wellington – to whose foresight and good taste we owe this most elegant of all British Embassies – would have enjoyed the day. For both knew a good horse when they saw one and, much as they admired the qualities of the French, neither was averse to teaching them an occasional sharp lesson, sporting or otherwise.

In most Arc de Triomphes, however, the lesson has been the other way round and even mammoth doses of bottled courage could not altogether remove the painful memories of Sir Ivor, Park Top, Nijinsky and other high hopes left shattered in front of the Longchamp stands.

Meeting Ian Balding at the entrance of the tree-lined pre-parade ring I enquired anxiously if all was well. 'He's fine,' said Ian and, pointing to where Mill Reef had just walked in, 'there – how do you think he looks?' There followed an awkward pause because, to tell the truth, I thought he looked pretty awful. And Ian now admits that, in the few minutes between being saddled and entering the paddock Mill Reef's appearance had altered very much for the worse. 'It's as though he was holding his breath,' Geoff Lewis says and that is a precise description. The greater the nervous tension and excitement the more Mill Reef seemed to 'tuck himself up' at such moments and now, although he had slept and eaten quite normally since arriving in France, big four-year-olds like Caro, Hallez, Ortis and Ramsin made him look fragile and insignificant. 'Behind his girth and down his quarters,' I wrote at the time, 'Mill Reef had run up undeniably light. And the awful question asked itself – might not what looked like relaxation be in reality the apathy of a horse "gone off the boil"?'

But at least he *was* relaxed and in fact his mind, for a while, seems to have been on something far removed from racing. There are horse-chestnut trees in the pre-parade ring at Longchamp, and, spotting some particularly juicy conkers on the ground Tom Reilly asked John Hallum to stop a

moment while he collected a few. At the first time of asking
Mill Reef did not take kindly to this interruption but then
he saw what Tom was doing. 'And from then on,' John says,
'everytime we reached a conker he stopped of his own accord.
In the end when Tom had plenty it was a job to get him
past them.' You can call it fanciful if you please but this
hardly sounds like a horse overawed by the occasion. When
Mill Reef entered the main paddock the crowd clapped and
cheered. He paused for a moment but then walked on quite
unperturbed.

Twelve months earlier, for Nijinsky, beset on every side
by a snapping, flashing pack of photographers, the paddock
before the Arc had been a dreadful nerve-racking ordeal
which may well have made the difference between victory
and defeat. Now, to their credit, the French Authorities tried
very hard to enforce a rule against photographers, and just
in case, the large and muscular figure of William Hastings-
Bass was added to Mill Reef's bodyguard.

Then the waiting was over. Geoff Lewis whose day had
begun triumphantly with a victory on Sweet Revenge in the
Prix de l'Abbaye de Longchamp swung up on to Mill Reef's
back, smiling and at least outwardly quite calm. And soon,
as they cantered past the stands, greeted by a cheer in which
many different tongues were mingled, all my doubts about
the little horse's well-being seemed mere craven pessimism.
Neck stretched far out as usual he bounded eagerly away
and as those wiry quarters bunched and sprang their
abnormal power was clear again for all to see.

Unlike Nijinsky the year before, Mill Reef had an ideal
draw – No. 7 in a field of eighteen. Both the Prix du Cadran
winner Ramsin and his pacemaker Ossian were drawn between him and the rail but the brilliant filly Pistol Packer,
unbeaten in her last five races and generally regarded as Mill
Reef's most dangerous rival, was badly drawn, 18 on the
wide outside.

In working out his tactics beforehand Geoff Lewis had

sought the advice of George Bridgland who won the first post-war Epsom Derby on Pearl Diver and knows Longchamp as well as any man alive. 'Never be out of the first half dozen,' Bridgland told him and, remembering Lester Piggot's tribulations on Nijinsky and Park Top Geoff decided to follow his advice.

The American five-year-old One For All was actually first to break but a moment later Ossian dashed clear with Ramsin at his heels and although Mill Reef took a rather stronger hold than usual Geoff was easily able to settle on the rails behind them. Sharapour, Lester Piggott's mount, Hallez and Ortis were all in the leading group, but while Mill Reef lost a length or two as they swung downhill towards the turn he was never at any stage worse than sixth.

Peter Scott, writing afterwards in *Stud and Stable*, gave a breakdown of the time in the four fastest races run in recent years over the Longchamp mile-and-a-half – the Arcs of Mill Reef, Sassafras and Levmoss and the Prix Vermelle won by Highest Hopes.

	Mill Reef	Sassafras	Highest Hopes	Levmoss
2400m–2000m	27.60	29.10	28.30	28.70
2000m–1600m	25.20	23.50	24.30	24.80
1600m–1200m	26.70	24.40	24.40	24.60
1200m– 800m	21.70	23.80	23.60	23.70
800m– 400m	22.60	24.40	24.50	23.70
400m– 200m	12.10	12.20	12.00	11.50
200m– Finish	12.40	12.30	12.10	12.00
	2m 28.30	2m 29.70	2m 29.20	2m 29.00

What these figures show is that while Ossian set a blistering gallop for the first two hundred metres the pace was comparatively 'slow' for the next eight hundred. But then, six furlongs from home in our language, the race was on in deadly earnest and, as Peter says, it seems fair to question whether the next half mile, mainly downhill and round a gentle right-hand bend, has ever been covered faster in any twelve furlong race at Longchamp. It was during these four crucial furlongs that Geoff Lewis faced his most difficult tactical dilemma and it was here too that we in the stands had our only serious moment of doubt. But just bear in mind, as you read the next few paragraphs, that the incidents described took place at an average speed of more than forty miles an hour.

Halfway round the bend, foreseeing that Ossian was bound to tire, Geoff eased out from the rail behind him. His intention then was to challenge outside the leaders but now between him and the daylight he craved there appeared the implacable poker face of Lester Piggott. It was not, at that particular moment, the most welcome sight in all the world. For Lester, who has always been a little hard of hearing can, when he chooses, be stone deaf .

'At times like that,' said Geoff, 'you just don't bother talking. So as Lester kicked for home I pulled back in behind him.' It was, he has told me since, the only time in all his fourteen rides on Mill Reef that he felt himself in a false and dangerous position. And to us in the stands, as the familiar white nose band vanished completely behind a line of nodding heads and waving whips (Hallez, Ortis and Sharapour were roughly in line abreast), the danger was agonizingly apparent.

For both Ortis and Sharapour were already beaten horses and, as they began to weaken, Freddie Head drove Pistol Packer up on Hallez's left. If Geoff had stayed where he was the filly would have got first run, and Mill Reef would have had to come round behind both her and Hallez before beginning his challenge. To escape from such predicaments a horse needs three things, courage, acceleration – and luck. The hero of this story has never been short of the first two and now he got the share he needed of the third. For as Ortis fell back he hung a little towards the inside rail and between him and Hallez the longed-for gap appeared. It can't have been very wide and it certainly would not have stayed open very long. But for Mill Reef at this, the climax of his whole career, it was enough. One moment we were searching anxiously along the jumbled line of colours, the next they parted and, like some projectile thrown from an angry crowd, a small, dark, utterly unmistakable figure detached itself.

For what happened in the next twenty seconds or so I have had to rely on films and photographs because at the time the Press Box, full of supposedly hard-headed scribes, exploded into something very like hysteria. It is never easy at the best of times to analyse a finish while screaming your head off, and even harder when a large French lady is waving her parasol under your nose.

But we know now that Geoff, feeling rightly that it was now or never, hit Mill Reef just once, for the first time since the Two Thousand Guineas. We know that, for perhaps a furlong, Pistol Packer hung on gallantly at his quarters – and we know that he trebled his lead over her in the final hundred yards with the same crescendo of power which had decorated the finishes of so many of his races. We knew even then, as he passed the post, that Europe's richest race had been superbly won and a few moments later we knew that the time was a clear-cut record of 2 m. 28.3 s.

As Mill Reef pulled up another race was on – between four of his closest friends, half mad with excitement and each determined if possible to be the first to welcome their hero home. Tom Reilly won – employing his own special mixture of weight, muscle and Irish blarney. But Bill Palmer who, unknown to Ian, had come to Lonchamp with a party organised by the *Sporting Life,* went over a seven-foot iron railing as if it was an upturned dandy-brush and was only robbed of the verdict by a posse of highly suspicious gendarmes. John Hallum and Bill Jennings were close behind. So the six of them came back in triumph, forcing their way through a jostling, cheering crowd to the paddock where Mr and Mrs Mellon, Ian, Emma and her mother were waiting. I wrote shortly afterwards that no flat-race course in my experience ever contained more happy ahd delighted human beings than Longchamp that afternoon and, although Brigadier Gerard's last race produced an ecstatic scene at Newmarket, I have certainly not seen anything like it since. For although the French racing crowd can be unfair, capricious and even cruel they know true excellence when they see it and care not a jot from whence it comes.

'Mille Bravos pour Mill Reef,' said *Figaro* next day and *Le Parisien* stated flatly that the winner had 'formally proved himself the best horse in the world'. But perhaps the most significant headline of them all was that of *Paris-Turf*. 'Comme Sea Bird II – mais plus vite,' it ran; that 'plus vite' referred to the seven seconds by which, admittedly on faster going, Mill Reef had bettered Sea Bird's time. No one of course can claim that he was a better horse but it is eloquent proof of the impression left by his victory that French racing's own trade paper should make such a comparison.

The 1971 Prix de l'Arc de Triomphe was the first in this century to be attended by the French President. Mr and Mrs Mellon, Ian and Geoff Lewis were taken up to be congratulated by Monsieur and Madame Pompidou. After the Derby Geoff had been presented to the Queen and as he sat down a little wearily to change in the Longchamp weighing room, someone enquired who he would like to meet next. 'My old woman – if only if I can find her,' Geoff replied and, quite soon, I'm glad to say, he did.

It takes two to win a horse-race and I apologise to Geoff for leaving so late in Mill Reef's story my tribute to the enormous part played in it by his jockey. Perfection is a big word which should be sparingly used but nothing else will do to describe Geoff Lewis's riding of Mill Reef in his last four races as a three-year-old. Apart from two brief moments at Epsom and Longchamp – neither of which could be avoided and each of which was coolly and skilfully dealt with – the little horse was never once in anything less than a perfect position. He was never baulked, he never became unbalanced, he never lay out of his ground and all his challenges were launched at the right place and the right time. That is praise as high as any jockey can wish and by the end of 1971 the cheerful ex page boy, born in Wales but a Cockney at heart, had established himself firmly among the world's finest practitioners of a difficult profession.

As Mill Reef walked calmly away to be washed down, his admirers from a dozen different countries set about celebrating his victory as it deserved. Before the race William Hastings-Bass had distributed small gold and black lapel buttons bearing the legend 'Mill Reef' and now, swilling champagne in the dying autumn sunlight of a perfect day, we wore them with redoubled pride. It was one of those times when the frivolous artificial game of racing seemed to be transformed and lifted far above its usual humdrum self.

Before leaving the Arc Mill Reef's victims must be given their due, especially the two gallant fillies who followed him home. Pistol Packer, and Cambrizzia whom she beat by a length and a half, had met twice before that year and now they reproduced their previous form almost to a yard. Caro who finished fourth a neck behind Cambrizzia got just over a length closer to Mill Reef than he had in the Eclipse and ran his usual admirable race. He was followed home by Hallez, the good English colt Royalty, and Bourbon who both behaved and ran a great deal better than in the Derby.

No serious excuses were offered for any beaten horse. Despite her unfavourable draw Pistol Packer, as we have seen, had been very nearly level with Mill Reef three furlongs out. Tragically her career was ended by an accident when pulling up at the finish of a race next season but she was without doubt a wonderful filly, and Cambrizzia who came from a long way back in the Arc to finish faster than anything bar the winner, was only slightly her inferior.

X-rays of the broken leg:

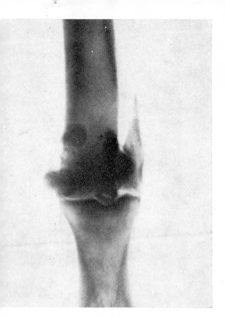

Before the operation

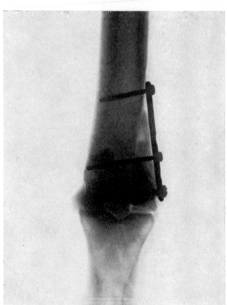

After

The surgery completed

Learning to live in plaster (with John Hallum)

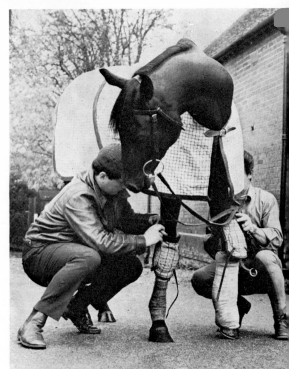

Learning to walk again (Ian Balding left)

One last footnote should be added. It is that in both Geoff Lewis's and Lester Piggott's opinion Mill Reef was not, in the Arc, as good as he had been in the Eclipse and the King George VI and Queen Elizabeth Stakes. There is no way of proving this, but Caro's running, over a distance probably just beyond his best, is some slight confirmation. And Lester is particularly emphatic on the point. 'He was over the top, I'm sure of it,' he says, 'and to win *that* race as he did – well that has to be some racehorse.' The great jockey does not give praise lightly and his words are worth remembering. They are a fitting final comment on Mill Reef's supreme achievement, more significant to my mind that all the many other superlatives which as he returned to England were showered on his head.

CHAPTER THIRTEEN

The Prix Ganay

Some breeding experts – Brigadier Gerard's owner John Hislop among them – believe that the present dominance of American-bred horses in Europe is due at least partly to precocity. Citing, for instance, Nijinsky – who certainly had the physique of a four-year-old when he won the Derby – they argue that the Classic three-year-old tests come too early for slower-developing European horses and give their transatlantic rivals an 'unfair' advantage.

There may well be some truth in this, though I would note in passing that no observer of the 1971 Two Thousand Guineas field could possibly claim that Mill Reef looked a more 'mature' specimen than either Brigadier Gerard or My Swallow. But in any case although some American horses are undoubtedly precocious by European standards I do not think it either fair or logical to conclude from this, as some exponents of the theory have, that the same horses are certain or even likely to deteriorate with age. It is true of course that Sea Bird II, Sir Ivor and Nijinsky were none of them given a chance to confirm their excellence as four-year-olds but that does not prove that they would all have failed to do so. Plenty of European 'champions' have been retired to stud with equal or even greater haste, plenty more have failed to train on; and the American record books are full of horses who race successfully year after year, often running as many times in one season as most Europeans do in a life time.

In my own view the present American supremacy is based

on three main foundations. One is certainly top-class blood imported regardless of cost from Europe over a period of many years; another is the comparatively ruthless way in which they train and race their horses, running them hard and often in contests where the main tactical principle is often 'the devil take the hindmost'.

It is a system in which only tough sound animals can hope to survive – the perfect basis in fact for selective breeding. I also believe, that the Americans, most of whose important races are run over a mile-and-a-quarter or less, have achieved an ideal blend of speed and stamina. Of course they produce much short-running stock but the best of their products, when trained to relax and conserve energy in the European manner, have not only enough stamina to last our own championship mile-and-a-half but also enough speed to beat horses bred on traditional European middle distance lines. And if, at the same time, such horses have the precocity to win in the top class as two-year-olds over five and six furlongs – well, good luck to them. I can see nothing very undesirable about that.

There is, on the other hand, no reason why the present wave of transatlantic domination should last for ever, any more than did the post-war superiority enjoyed by horses bred and trained in France. Bloodstock breeding is now such a polyglot international business that champions will surely be bred on both sides of the Atlantic. In the meanwhile there is little to be gained by underrating the wonderful results achieved by American breeders. Happily, thanks to men like Mr Mellon, we have been privileged to enjoy watching some of those results in action and, even more happily, some of them are now standing at stud in Europe. Our aim should surely be to capitalise on that good fortune, and to combine what is best in American racing with what is best in our own.

Nevertheless the theory referred to above is still quite widely held and one of Mill Reef's main tasks in 1972 was to disprove it, at least on his own behalf. Fate, as it happened did not allow him to accomplish that task completely but the one chance he had was seized, so to speak, with both hands. It came at Longchamp on 30 April, 1972 in the £30,000 Prix Ganay.

After a winter spent as I have described it in chapter eight Mill Reef went back into strong training at the beginning of March. I can testify myself that he looked magnificent and by common consent of all who rode him he felt better and stronger than ever before. It was on 8 March in fact that Geoff Lewis, down at Kingsclere to ride him a strong canter for five furlongs, so narrowly escaped being decanted (see page 52). And just over a month later Mill Reef went to Newbury for a public work out before racing on the day of the Greenham Stakes. Two old friends, Aldie and Morris Dancer, were there to keep him company and although the time for one-and-a-quarter miles on soft ground was a good deal slower than his work before the Arc both Ian Balding and everyone else in the large and fascinated crowd were more than satisfied. A furlong or so from the finish Geoff Lewis only had to let out an inch of rein and Mill Reef who was giving at least a stone to both his companions pulled cheerfully twelve lengths clear. Later the same afternoon Martinmas won the Greenham, so Ian went back to Kingsclere a contented man.

The rest of Mill Reef's preparation for the Ganay passed off without a hitch but this was nevertheless a worrying time for his trainer. Before the flat-race season began Ian had been warned by the Racing Security Services of a persistent under-world rumour that Mill Reef was to be kidnapped. It may sound now like something out of a Dick Francis thriller but Ian quite rightly took the warning very seriously indeed. The block in which Mill Reef lived, already fitted with burglar alarms, was turned into a miniature electronic fortress. Ian's assistant secretary Peter Harbinson kept watch for long periods in the middle of the day from a new office specially designed and strategically placed overlooking Mill Reef's box. At night nothing larger than a mouse could move about the yard without setting off an alarm in Bill Palmer's bedroom. One night, in fact, while checking the system, Bill found to his horror that the bells were not working and, suspecting the worst telephoned Ian. But in the neck of time before the whole Hampshire Police Force could be mobilized the culprit was discovered. It was a bird who, by pecking through a vital wire had crippled the whole complicated system.

Apart from extra security no special measures were taken this time to ease Mill Reef's passage to France, but despite a delay caused by Merry Slipper's reluctance to board the aeroplane the flight took less out of him than any of his two previous journeys.

The field for the Ganay was, in one respect, a disappointment, for Pistol Packer, effortless winner of her first race as a four-year-old, had been badly struck into as she pulled up after it. In her absence Mill Reef's opponents were certainly no world beaters but most of them had won good races and one, Amadou had run Caro to three-quarters of a length in the same contest twelve months earlier.

The comparative weakness of the opposition eased Geoff Lewis's tactical problems, and this was just as well for his peace of mind. For weighing room gossip had it that a plan existed to 'take care of' Mill Reef during the race. The rumour was almost certainly slanderous to the jockeys involved but Geoff decided to take no chances. As Merry Slipper set off in front he steered Mill Reef to the outside and, settling down in fourth place kept his opponents where he could see them : between him and the rails.

A film had been commissioned on Mill Reef's fortunes in 1972 and this was the first occasion on which its cameras were in action. For the venture's racing adviser Brough Scott, surrounded by sceptical technicians to whom he had been singing Mill Reef's praises, the Prix Ganay was a fairly nervous experience. Brough remembers – and so do I – one awful moment soon after half way when Mill Reef appeared to be well and truly off the bit. 'Oh God,' we both thought 'perhaps he hasn't trained on after all.' But the agony did not last long.

For this, as Geoff Lewis has since explained to me, was precisely Mill Reef's ideal situation, a race on soft ground run so fast that he dropped his bit completely and cruised along relaxed while the others struggled to keep up. And now as they began the gradual downhill turn for home he got tired of waiting. 'Something came up beside us,' Geoff recalls, 'and he just took off.' In a dozen strides, like a sheep-dog herding a dilatory flock, the little horse shot round and past his field. It was much sooner than Geoff had meant to move but 'what the hell' he thought, and kicked briefly for home.

Even allowing for the limitations of the opposition the next twenty seconds or so were unforgettable. In a hundred yards a yawning gap began to open behind Mill Reef and fully a furlong from home Geoff dropped his hands. But this, as we have seen, has never discouraged his companion and now, drawing relentlessly further and further ahead he pulled his way past the post. The photographs facing page 65 show more clearly than any words the extraordinary rate at which, in every yard of that last furlong, he left his floundering hard-ridden rivals. They also show, I think, that the judge's verdict of ten lengths must come high on any list of historic understatements. Fifteen would be a conservative estimate and twenty little exaggeration.

The Longchamp crowd had started cheering soon after Mill Reef hit the front and now, although few of them could have got rich on a *pari mutuel* price of ten to one on, they gave him the sort of welcome usually reserved for winners of the Prix de l'Arc de Triomphe.

'I have seen some good horses in my time,' said Geoff Watson, the highly experienced trainer of Amadou, who finished second, 'but never one like that'. And M Jean Romanet, already one of Mill Reef's most fervent admirers, went even further. 'That,' he said simply, 'is the best horse I have seen at Longchamp.'

Racehorses of 1972, realistic as usual, puts the Ganay in a rather colder perspective by pointing out that Amadou (who had incidentally finished at least ten lengths behind Brigadier Gerard in the Champion Stakes the previous year) could not win another race in France until November. But even its hard-headed observers called Mill Reef's performance 'the most spectacular victory seen since Sea Bird's Arc de Triomphe'.

Anyway, whatever the precise value of the form, Mill Reef's running in the Prix Ganay was unmistakably that of a horse at the peak of condition and power. Throughout the last two furlongs, without encouragement or competition he was galloping purely for the fun of it – doing the thing he loved best and doing it supremely well. I do not think it can be denied, in fact, that the result of the Prix Ganay is conclusive proof that on 30 April, 1972 Mill Reef, as a four-year-old, was at least as good as at any previous stage of his career.

CHAPTER FOURTEEN

The Race That Never Was

Three weeks after Mill Reef came back in triumph from the Ganay Brigadier Gerard reappeared at Newbury. He won the Lockinge Stakes comfortably if not by his standards spectacularly from the three-year-old Grey Mirage and nine days later went to Sandown for the Westbury Stakes.

This race is run over the full course and distance of the Eclipse, by common consent the most likely battlefield for the Brigadier's second meeting with Mill Reef. As every soldier knows time spent in reconnaissance is seldom wasted but in fact Brigadier Gerard found rather stronger opposition at Sandown than a scouting party likes to meet. Receiving a stone, the very useful Ballyhot set out to make all the running and, when collared a furlong from home fought back with quite remarkable tenacity. Joe Mercer had to rouse the Brigadier in earnest to win by half a length and no one watching the race could be certain that he had very much more to spare.

There was of course no line of form to connect this performance with Mill Reef's in the Ganay. But I think it fair to say that of those who had seen both races there were very few unconnected with either horse who did not at that time expect Mill Reef to come out best if, as both sides intended, the two of them met in the Eclipse.

For both, however, one more race was planned – the Coronation Cup for Mill Reef and the Prince of Wales's Stakes at Royal Ascot for Brigadier Gerard. And before 8

June when the Coronation Cup was run two ominous things had happened. On 29 May ten days before Epsom Mill Reef went back to the 'left hand side' gallop over which he had so encouraged Ian Balding at the same stage before the Derby. Aldie was there again but this time the third horse in the gallop was Martinmas, winner of the Greenham Stakes that year and second in the Irish Two Thousand Guineas. Ridden by Paul Cook Mill Reef carried 9 st. 12 lb., Martinmas 8 st. 13 lb. and Aldie 8 st. 2 lb. The weather had been so foul all week that Mill Reef had missed a couple of gallops; now, although a strong wind was still blowing, Ian decided to go ahead.

His gallop sheets record the result : 'Martinmas best but tired, Mill Reef struggled, *not himself*. Aldie worked very well'. The time on soft ground was 2 m. 25 s. and Ian wrote below it, *'very hard work'*.

At the time, quite understandably, the trainer put Mill Reef's poor showing down to the rest he had been given since the Ganay, to those missed gallops and to general lack of fitness. Two days later, going seven furlongs with Bright Beam, he was 'best but not great' and four days after that he covered the same mile and a quarter in 2 m. 28.5 s. : 'easily best but *blew for a long time*'. Ian Balding's anxiety shows in those last words – and in the fact that on 5 June he got Geoff Lewis down to ride Mill Reef for six furlongs up the Valley. The horse did not blow for quite so long this time and while neither jockey nor trainer was altogether happy they consoled themselves with the thought that the opposition seemed sure to be weak at Epsom – indeed that Mill Reef might even have a walk-over.

But then on Derby Day there came a second even direr warning of which, to be wise after the event, they should perhaps have taken notice. An hour after the Derby Martinmas started a 5–4 favourite for the Diomed Stakes and finished last of all. It was clearly so far from his proper form that something had to be wrong. On the other hand

Aldie made every yard of the running to win the Daily Mirror Handicap and in any case Mill Reef was already declared to run. There was nothing visibly amiss with him, and he had only three rivals in the Coronation Cup, including his own pacemaker Bright Beam.

He had beaten both the other two before but now one of them, Brigadier Gerard's stable companion Homeric, was to give his supporters their first really anxious moment since the Two Thousand Guineas. Racing down into Tattenham Corner – just about where he had done Geoff Lewis such a favour in the Derby twelve months earlier – Joe Mercer suddenly 'kicked' for home. Homeric went maybe three lengths clear but Geoff had not then asked Mill Reef to chase him and, when he did, the answer came smoothly enough.

Just under two furlongs out surging easily up alongside Homeric Milll Reef looked sure to come clear away. But then, unbelievably, Geoff began to ride. A second later he pulled his whip through to the left hand and still Homeric hung on gallantly at Mill Reef's girths. There he stayed to the end, and although Geoff never actually hit Mill Reef neither he nor anyone else suggests that the little horse could have pulled out much more than the neck by which he won.

This was of course a major propaganda victory for Brigadier Gerard's admirers and two races at Royal Ascot made them feel even better. In the Prince of Wales's Stakes the Brigadier returned to his spectacular best, slamming the subsequent Irish Derby winner Steel Pulse by five majestic lengths; and in the Hardwicke Stakes, Homeric was made to look decidedly one-paced by Selhurst and Frascati.

With the Eclipse Stakes only a fortnight ahead the whole balance of power had suddenly been reversed. Some of the bookmakers who had been offering five to two against Brigadier Gerard now made him a narrow odds on favourite to beat Mill Reef and even the latter's most convinced adherents felt their confidence distinctly shaken.

Mill Reef was tested in every conceivable way after the Coronation Cup but the only noticeable after-effect was that he had lost much more weight than usual – thirty pounds more, for instance, than after the Ganay. But his blood count was normal (it remained so throughout the year), he was eating well and when cantered six days after Epsom he looked pretty much his old exuberant self.

If you count his narrow victory over Hecla in the Imperial Stakes the Coronation Cup was only the second time in Mill Reef's whole career that he ran clearly and unaccountably below his best. And it was not until the autumn of 1972 that Ian Balding was able to put together a convincing explanation. It is based, securely in my opinion, on two separate pieces of evidence.

The first materialised at Longchamps in October when Homeric, who was by that time trained in France, took the lead two furlongs from home in the Prix de l'Arc de Triomphe with the race apparently at his mercy. A few strides later, as his rider Maurice Philipperon confirmed afterwards, he broke down badly; even so it was only by two lengths and half a length that San San and Rescousse managed to beat him. The sixteen unplaced horses that day were, as usual in the Arc, a cross-section of the best in Europe. They included Brigadier Gerard's only conqueror Roberto, Parnell who had run the Brigadier so close at Ascot, the French Derby winner Hard To Beat, the English St Leger winner Boucher and the Irish Derby winner Steel Pulse.

This was admittedly far and away the best performance of Homeric's career. But nevertheless as he hobbled dead lame into the unsaddling enclosure the thoughts of many present went back to the Coronation Cup – and to the little horse who, equally lame, was languishing in his box at Kingsclere. For it was now clear that to beat Homeric by a neck, as Mill Reef did at Epsom, might not after all have been so mediocre a performance.

The second piece of evidence lay on Ian Balding's desk not long after the Arc. It took the form of an analyst's report from the Equine Research Centre at Newmarket. All sort of tests, as we have seen, were made on Mill Reef after Epsom and although his blood count was normal an exhaustive analysis of some swabs taken from his nose and throat took three months to produce. But now the report was unequivocal. In June 1972 – and almost certainly when he ran at Epsom – Mill Reef was suffering from Rhinopneumonitis.

Though mainly a scourge of brood mares, in whom it causes abortion, this is one of several viruses which has crippled so many English stables during the past decade. Its chief symptom in a mature racehorse is sudden premature exhaustion under stress; in other words it causes outwardly healthy animals to weaken just when, towards the finish of a race, they are asked for extra effort. Horses, unlike humans, can only breathe through their noses, not their mouths. Any form of cold or cattarrh is therefore a dreadful handicap, certain to make a horse run out of steam the moment real pressure is applied. That is precisely what Mill Reef did two furlongs from home in the Coronation Cup and in the light of this knowledge – taken together with Homeric's form in the Prix de l'Arc de Triomphe – it seems fair to guess that, so far from being a 'disgrace' or 'failure' Mill Reef's last race may also have been among his bravest.

None of this, alas, was known to Ian Balding in June 1972, but even if Mill Reef seemed all right it was all too painfully clear that many of his other horses had something very wrong with them. Peter Scott-Dunn, watching a morning's work not long after Epsom noticed that several supposedly fit horses were blowing abnormally hard and towards the middle of June ominous wet noses began to sppear throughout the yard. On 27 June, with the Eclipse only ten days off, Mill Reef left his evening feed almost totally untouched. Next morning he was running a temperature of

102 and Ian had no choice but to announce that the 'race of the century' would have to be postponed. In fact, as it transpired next day, that temperature was probably caused more by an abscess in Mill Reef's mouth than, as both Ian and Peter Scott-Dunn assumed, by the virus. But the result was much the same. There could be no question of sending him up against Brigadier Gerard at anything less than his absolute peak and perhaps the abscess was a blessing in disguise.

It did not seem that way when on the night and morning before the Eclipse hours of heavy rain produced at Sandown precisely the sort of going Mill Reef loved and his great rival hated. Although the opposition was, by his high standards, second-rate Brigadier Gerard's owner and trainer pondered long and hard before deciding to run. And I do not think there is any doubt that, had a fit Mill Reef been in the field they would, with the conditions as they were, have decided otherwise. As it was, gallant as ever, Brigadier Gerard struggled home, but only by a laborious length from Gold Rod, a horse to whom on better going he was infinitely superior.

Ian Balding toyed briefly with the idea of training Mill Reef for the King George VI and Queen Elizabeth Stakes – but only very briefly. There was, or seemed to be, plenty of time, and a new richly sponsored mile-and-a-quarter race, the Benson and Hedges Gold Cup, due to be run at York on 15 August was an obviously suitable alternative.

So for most of July Mill Reef was rested and as he strolled quietly round the tracks and hedgerows near Park House Brigadier Gerard went to Ascot to run what was, in my opinion, one of his best and most courageous races. For I do not believe that the Brigadier truly stayed a mile-and-a-half, if by 'truly stayed' you understand 'was as good at that distance as a mile-and-quarter or less'. It was class not stamina that carried him past the out-and-out stayer Parnell – and courage that kept him there, hanging so sharply to his right that for thirteen agonising minutes it seemed possible that his unbeaten record might be lost in the Stewards' room.

But all was well and as Mill Reef started gentle work at Kingsclere with the Benson and Hedges in view the 'Race of the Century' seemed to be on once more.

On 22 July, having his first serious gallop for a month, Mill Reef left Merry Slipper standing over a mile. Three days later he worked even better with Bright Beam and on the 29th, back on 'the left hand side' with Aldie and Bright Beam, he finished the mile-and-a-quarter running away. 'In great form,' Ian wrote on his gallop sheet and as he left the Downs that morning the horizon looked clear at last.

But fate had not relented after all. Halfway through that work Paul Cook had felt Mill Reef falter for a stride or so and was not surprised to find on pulling up that he had lost his off fore shoe. It was not until evening stables that the baleful results of this very ordinary accident materialised.

Then, however, they were all too clear. The shoe must have twisted before coming off and a ridge across Mill Reef's near fore tendon showed where it had struck him. He was not lame and antiphlogistine poultices applied over the week-end brought the leg back to normal. It came up again after only one brief canter on Monday morning but after six days walking and treatment with an ultra-sonic machine (administered by Peter Scott-Dunn's wife) all trace of the injury disappeared.

Mr Mellon had of course been kept constantly informed of all those developments and had as usual borne this disappointment philosophically. But when on 9 August Ian Balding had to tell him that Mill Reef had pulled a muscle in his quarters it must have seemed the last straw. No one knows how this disaster happened but the little horse was probably over-fresh from lack of work and somehow managed to get 'cast' and injure himself in his box. Mr Mellon's reaction was to ask if his own American Veterinary adviser Charles Allen (chief racecourse vet at Aqueduct) could come over to assess

the situation. Ian agreed at once and Mr Allen arrived on
12 August. His verdict was that the tendon injury had been
of no account but that it would be madness in all the circumstances to attempt the Benson and Hedges Gold Cup.
He added that in his opinion Mill Reef was perfectly well in
himself and should be ready for a race in a month's time
preparatory to the Prix de l'Arc de Triomphe.

There was, as it happened, just such a race in the Calendar
because, with a little judicious prodding from Ian, and partly
perhaps with a view to attracting Brigadier Gerard, the Ascot
Authority had reduced the distance of the Cumberland Lodge
Stakes from twelve furlongs to ten. This was a Group 3
Pattern Race and the alteration of its conditions without
consulting the Pattern Committee caused a certain amount
of justifiable irritation at the time. But that is another story.

Worth only £3,000 to the winner the Cumberland Lodge
never had much chance, in fact, of becoming the 'Race of
the Century' but it would have been a perfect final gallop
for Mill Reef's second attempt on the Arc. That, anyway,
was the plan when Charles Allen left Kingsclere for America,
and a fortnight later when Mill Reef did his first strong
canter Ian Balding's only worry was that he still seemed a
little thick in his wind.

It was accordingly with a heartfelt sigh of relief that he
heard and saw the little horse sail past him on the morning
of 30 August breathing clean and moving free. For about
thirty seconds Ian was, for the first time in more than two
months, an entirely happy man – and the savage blow that
followed was all the more difficult to bear.

CHAPTER FIFTEEN

Disaster – and Triumph

Ian Balding's first thought that morning was that Mill Reef must have split a pastern. That, for a four-year-old, would have been quite bad enough but the truth, as a brief inspection told him, was far worse.

In fact, four separate bones in Mill Reef's near foreleg were gravely injured and as a result the whole fetlock joint was left totally unstable. The order in which the injuries occurred can only be a matter of opinion and, in fact, the first warning John Hallum got was a loud crack almost certainly from Mill Reef's cannon bone. But this, the most serious injury of all, may itself have been caused by the total collapse of the inner sesamoid, one of two small bones on either side of the fetlock. If the sesamoid shattered first, the joint would probably have dislocated outwards, throwing an abnormal and insupportable burden on the cannon bone. As that happened, according to this theory, the rim at the top of the long pastern-bone crumpled, the other sesamoid cracked in two and, either then or earlier, a triangular piece nearly three inches long broke off the cannon bone, driving upwards into the Medulla and splintering as it did so. The fragments caused by this collision fell down into the crack and would, if not removed, have hindered or prevented reunion of the fracture.

None of this, of course, was known to Ian Balding or John Hallum as they stood in despair that morning, waiting for

Farewell party at Kingsclere

MILL REEF

MILL REEF (BAY, 1968)	NEVER BEND	NASRULLAH	NEARCO	PHAROS
				NOGARA
			MUMTAZ BEGUM	BLENHEIM
				MUMTAZ MAHAL
		LALUN	DJEDDAH	DJEBEL
				DJEZIMA
			BE FAITHFUL	BIMELECH
				BLOODROOT
	MILAN MILL	PRINCEQUILLO	PRINCE ROSE	ROSE PRINCE
				INDOLENCE
			COSQUILLA	PAPYRUS
				QUICK THOUGHT
		VIRGINIA WATER	COUNT FLEET	REIGH COUNT
				QUICKLY
			RED RAY	HYPERION
				INFRA RED

His new home, the National Stud

At the National Stud

Free again

the horsebox which Mrs Hastings had hurried down to summon.

John's first memory is, as I have said, that dreadful crack, followed at once by a headlong plunge which pitched him up Mill Reef's neck. Even then, on three legs, instinct and momentum carried the horse along for fifty yards and in the end, John had to fling himself off to bring him to a standstill. The wait that followed was agony for both men, but Mill Reef, not yet in serious pain, stood quietly resting his leg and munching grass. He had still to master the art of walking, though, and it took him nearly half an hour to cover the twenty yards to the side of the gallop. By that time, Bill Palmer and Tom Reilly had the horsebox in position and to all four men, its lowered ramp looked horribly – perhaps impossibly – steep.

For a moment, as Mill Reef stood below it, Ian's eyes met Bill's across his quarters and the same unspoken question was in both their minds: what on earth to do next if he could not get up.

'You could almost see him working it out,' Ian says, 'thinking "I've got to get home somehow".' It was only the first of many strange and painful problems Mill Reef had to face in the next two months and he solved it with typical gallantry.

An awkward three-legged bound carried him on to the ramp and somehow, without assistance, he scrambled up it. But the effort cost him dear and now, shaking and sweating, his distress was heart-rendingly clear. Gently though Norton Jones, the Kingsclere driver, handled the box, the journey down from the gallops must have been a prolonged ordeal, but once in the yard, Mill Reef decided that his own box was the place to be. He hopped off the ramp at once across to the familiar door, and there at last relief was waiting.

Peter Scott-Dunn's assistant, Barry Williams, was ready with a pain-killing injection and as that took effect, he gently applied support bandaging to the injured leg. To him, as he told Ian Balding, the fetlock felt 'like a bag of marbles' and X-rays, taken two hours later by Peter Scott-Dunn's radiographer Mrs Grierson, confirmed that gloomy impression. So, as Barry Williams applied a second, much heavier, plaster of paris support, Ian set in motion the depressing business of telling Mr Mellon, announcing the news to the Press and assembling the experts on whose skill Mill Reef's life and future now depended.

Of the three men chosen, none, as it happened, was in England, but Peter Scott-Dunn hurried back from Germany where he had been attending the British Olympic team, Mr Mellon's own vet, Charles Allen, flew from America for the second time in three weeks, and Edwin James Roberts travelled down from Edinburgh, where he had been attending the BEVA Congress. Mr Roberts, who had only recently resigned from the Equine Research Centre at Newmarket, was and is famous all over the world for his pioneering work in veterinary surgery. When, on Saturday 2 September, these three men met at London Airport to examine the X-ray photographs of Mill Reef's leg, it was unanimously decided both that an operation was necessary and that he was the man to undertake it.

Ian Balding was adamant from the first that Mill Reef should not be moved again, so an operating theatre had to be improvised at Kingsclere. As luck would have it, Ian had recently started converting John Porter's old mess room (later used as a chapel) into a gymnasium for the lads. Light and heating had already been installed and the big airy room with its white-tiled walls and a door opening into Bill Palmer's house made an ideal hospital. In one half of it, an operating table was built to Mr Roberts's specifications: straw bales covered in polythene and supported by moveable wooden frames. Ian's brother-in-law, William Hastings-Bass, led the construction team and the frames were so designed that, after the operation, the other half of the room became a cosy straw-lined nest for Mill Reef's convalescence.

All that seemed a long way off when Mr Roberts began, with infinite care and ingenuity, to lay his plans for the operation. His own estimate of the odds was 3–1 on survival of some sort, but only even money a recovery complete enough to let the patient stand at stud.

About midday on 6 September, just a week after the accident, Mill Reef was given a sedative in his box and led slowly along a specially-laid 'tartan' rubber path to the operating theatre. Anaesthetising a horse is a horribly delicate business and, in case he should fall the wrong way, Ian, William, Bill Palmer John Hallum and Peter Scott-Dunn stood ready with three ropes attached to his neck, his girth and his tail. In fact, their help was hardly needed. Three minutes almost to the second after Mr Roberts had injected the initial dose of Thiopentone into Mill Reef's jugular vein, he gave the signal. So precise was his timing that, with only one gentle pull, Mill Reef subsided gracefully into the exact position planned. For the next seven hours his troubles were over; but those of the men around him had only just begun.

Throughout that afternoon, with only brief pauses for food, Mr Roberts worked unceasingly, assisted by his wife and Peter Scott-Dunn's partner, Anthony Ward, and watched with anxious fascination by Ian Balding and John Hallum. After cutting and folding back a flap of skin to reveal the injury, the surgeon's first task was to remove the fragments of cannon bone which were preventing a proper replacement of the fractured segment. This was then clamped in place and minutely checked for proper alignment. Mr Roberts had decided in advance that to treat the shattered sesamoids would take far too long and might in any case be unnecessary. The cannon bone was quite difficult enough and for its reinforcement he had chosen a modified buttress plate of the sort used to mend the broken legs of skiers, jockeys and the like. The plate was redesigned to take three screws – two of conventional size but one of the heaviest type available, as big as those used for pinning human hips.

This larger screw ran through the thickest part of the broken segment and into the cannon bone just above the fetlock joint. A second, small, screw secured the middle of the segment and a third anchored the top of the plate to the cannon bone above the fracture. All three screws were set at a slight angle to the leg because Mr Roberts calculated that by following the slope of the broken segment, he would lock it more firmly into place. (See photograph facing page 96).

Put like that, it all sounds reasonably simple, but holes had to be precisely drilled in advance for all three screws and, at one especially dangerous stage, the clamp holding the broken bone in place was removed while these checks were made. Again and again, X-rays (developed in Bill Palmer's bathroom) were taken to confirm the angle and depth of the drills and the alignment of the bone. And all the while, Mrs Roberts was constantly checking the patient's condition and adjusting the dose of anaesthetic. Mill Reef, in fact, had been – and remained throughout – so totally relaxed that the mixture of oxygen and Fluothane needed to keep him unconscious was only half as strong as that which a normal horse requires. Probably this confirms how right Ian Balding had been to insist on keeping him in his own box until the last possible moment, and certainly it improved his chances of recovery.

In another way too he was an exceptional patient, for when Mr Roberts came to drill the holes above his fetlock he found the bone harder than any in his experience. Since hardness and brittleness do sometimes go together this may explain how the bone came to break in the first place.

Ian and John scarcely left the box throughout the seven hours helping in various ways and stretching Mill Reef's hind legs every half an hour or so to maintain circulation. To them during the afternoon there was brought one cheerful piece of news; as his lifelong friend lay unconscious, Mill Reef's first galloping companion, Red Reef, won an apprentice race at Salisbury in Mr Mellon's colours. To the anxious men standing by the operating table, it seemed at least a hopeful omen.

And then at last it was finished. The final checks were made, the skin was stitched back into place and the surgeons applied a full-length plaster, reinforced with an iron splint specially forged by Tom Reilly. Just under an hour after Mr Roberts had completed his marathon task, Mill Reef recovered consciousness. It was a nerve-racking moment, because horses, particularly colts, often struggle to begin with; but with only a little help he rolled over and stood up at the first attempt.

The shock of such a prolonged operation puts a dreadful strain on a horse's constitution, especially on his liver, which has to deal with and dispose of all the accumulated poisons. Serious jaundice can easily set in and for the next three days and nights, struggling with a whole set of strange unpleasant sensations, Mill Reef faced yet another problem. Now, unable to bend his leg at all below the elbow, he had to work out an entirely new method of lying down. Watched day and night by Ian, John and Bill – and when they became exhausted, by volunteer apprentices and Mrs Hastings' two younger sons John and Simon – he tried first one way, then another. Once or twice, Ian offered a helping hand but Mill Reef would have none of that. It was something he had to do alone and in the end he did it. The very first time he was left unguarded, the watchers returned to find him prostrate fast asleep.

It was some time later, in fact, that Bill Palmer, coming unseen into the box, found how it had been done. Not knowing he was being watched, Mill Reef leant against the straw wall of his 'nest' and then, slowly, with infinite care, slid down it, thrusting out his injured leg. Just once, forgetting, he lay down on the bad side with the plaster under him – and had to be manhandled over before he could get up.

Eating very little but sustained by regular glucose 'drips'

and vitamin injections, he battled through the crucial post-operative period and quite soon, John Hallum was able to take him for short walks round the yard. Although the heavy plaster was several inches longer than his other leg, he soon got the knack of swinging it wide and, at this stage, was quite prepared to make full use of it.

From the first announcement of Mill Reef's injury a steady stream of good wishes, 'get well' cards, letters and presents had poured into Kingsclere. More than five hundred cards decorated the walls of his box before he left it and when I visited him one day not long after the operation there were enough peppermints, sugar and assorted goodies at his disposal to stock a fair-sized sweetshop. So many well-wishers sent money for anything he might need or want that, in the end Ian Balding used the surplus to buy a rocking-horse for the local orphanage. It's name, needless to say, is Mill Reef.

Like most horses he has always had an insatiable sweet tooth and long before, on journeys to the races, John Hallum and Bill Jennings found him a keen competitor for their sandwiches. Now, when Anne Palmer prepared snacks and breakfast for the apprentices who volunteered to guard him Mill Reef soon asked for – and got – a share of everything. His favourite breakfast, like many sensible civilised gentlemen, was toast, butter and marmalade.

When, forty days after the operation, the plaster was removed, the results were as good as anyone could possibly have hoped. The scar had healed so perfectly that the hair was already growing over it, the broken cannon bone had reunited firmly, the sesamoids were fused in fibrous tissue and the fetlock joint, though almost totally rigid, had not dropped. But now, with only a simple felt support in place of the plaster, Mill Reef no longer trusted his leg. He would only just put the tip of his toe to the ground and although John Hallum massaged them for hours, the triceps muscles of his forearm began to waste. Though prepared to tolerate almost any other form of treatment he still refused point blank to allow the muscle-building Faraday Machine.

A special shoe suggested by Peter Scott-Dunn and built up at the heel helped to some extent, but to make Mill Reef put weight on the injured leg it had in the end to be pulled forward with a rope tied to his pastern. This, as you can imagine, was an agonising period for the little horse's friends. Probably for the first time in his life, he was being forced to do something against his will, and no one at any given moment could be sure how much pain it was causing him. A major problem was replacing the shoes on his other feet, because a horse being shod has one leg in the air and must therefore put weight on the other three. When at last Tom Reilly managed it, Mill Reef was immediately more at ease and progress from then on was rapid. There remained the question of exercise and, at first to make him trot, John Hallum had to run round the covered ride with another lad (usually chosen by Ian because, like John, he was in the stable football team) running behind to provide the necessary encouragement.

Finally, and not without misgivings, Ian decided to let him loose and, as he grazed inside the covered side, the bridle was gently slipped off his head. For several minutes all was well – so much so that Ian left to watch the stable lads playing football in the next-door field. But as he arrived, the Kingsclere team scored a goal and a loud cheer echoed back into the covered ride. It may have simply frightened Mill Reef, but I prefer to think that it awakened memories of half-forgotten days – and of other excited human voices raised to shout him home. However that may be, its effect was explosive.

'Off he went,' John Hallum says, 'at a million miles an hour. We just didn't dare to look.'

But all was well, and for that brief moment, forgetting all the pain and fear of the past three months, Mill Reef was himself again. As he pulled up sharp and trotted back, there was scarcely a trace of lameness and had Mr Roberts been there he would have been a proud and happy man indeed.

Ever since the operation urgent discussions had been taking place in England and America and across the transatlantic telephone about Mill Reef's immediate future as a stallion. The vets were undecided whether he should go to stud at all in 1973 – and if so, how many mares he should be allowed to cover. In the end, with Ian Balding's strong support, Mr Mellon took the view that there was no great point in waiting. It was decided to limit Mill Reef's first season to twenty mares, a figure which later grew to twenty-three. Mr Mellon kept four nominations himself and gave one to Ian. One went to Lady Halifax and two to American, two to French and four to English breeders. For the remaining six the National Stud, where Mill Reef was to stand, held a ballot, for which there were eighty-five applications, on the basis of £10,000 for a live foal.

With the day of his departure approaching, Mill Reef held his last public audience one bright Sunday morning at Kingsclere. Nearly a hundred cars lined the road outside Park House and in the covered ride John Hallum led his friend through an eager crowd of admirers, young and old. Still lean and light after his long ordeal Mill Reef treated them as ever with perfect courtesy, nibbled titbits of various kinds and allowed himself to be patted, stroked and generally made a fuss of. I spoke to one lady that morning who had driven from Birmingham with two small children.

'We've never seen him before except on TV,' she said. 'And never even backed him once. But we *loved* him, you see, because he was so brave. Racing just won't be the same for us when he is gone.'

But he had to go and on the morning of 9 January, 1973, the lads at Kingsclere assembled with heavy hearts to watch him board the horsebox for the last time. For many of them too, nothing would ever be quite the same again.

When the box arrived at Newmarket, Ian Balding was waiting, more than slightly anxious about the impression Mill Reef would make on his new hosts. He need not have worried.

'He came down that ramp like a two-year-old,' Ian says, 'and stood looking round as if half expecting to see the starting stalls.'

As usual, excitement and novelty had set the adrenalin surging through Mill Reef's veins and as he walked to the new luxurious box with his name and pedigree blazoned on its door the old jaunty spring was back in his stride. A king had come to claim his new dominion, and no one watching him that day could have dreamt that this was a horse who, three months earlier, had hovered uneasily between life and death.

Epilogue

From the moment Mill Reef was first introduced to Village Gossip in the covering yard at the National Stud he took to his duties with an ideal mixture of eagerness and tact. At no time did his injured leg cause him any trouble and by the end of the season he had covered twenty-three mares of whom sixteen were tested in foal. Besides his old rival Hecla his mates in that first season included Park Top, Humble Duty, Highest Hopes and West Side Story.

On 14 June Edwin Roberts examined his patient and was able to give an entirely satisfactory report ending with these words.

'Mill Reef is a highly intelligent well-balanced animal and has retained his inquisitive interest in all that goes on around him. He has settled very well at the National Stud and an excellent understanding has been established between him and his handlers.

'The evidence of his mating performance and the findings of my examination indicate that he should be able to accept a full commitment of mares next season, and that his future ability at Stud is unlikely to be jeopardised by the condition of his left fore fetlock.'

A permaent syndication was accordingly arranged in which forty-one shares were distributed at a valuation of £50,000 each. Of these Mr Mellon retained eight and nine were bought by the Levy Board on behalf of the National Stud for use by British breeders. These will be allotted by ballot at a fee of £15,000 – £7,500 payable on 1 July and £7,500 payable on the birth of a live foal.

The remaining twenty-four shares were allotted to breeders from all over the world, nine based in France, five in England, five in America, four in Ireland and one in Italy.

Mr Mellon had always regarded Mill Reef as an international horse and was determined that his services should not be confined to any one country. The large number of French breeders in the list represents his gratitude for the two great prizes Mill Reef won in France and for the kindness and hospitality with which the horse and his entourage were always treated in that country.

By the end of his first covering season Mill Reef had matured into the magnificent specimen shown in the frontispiece of this book. His career had already depended on men of many different nationalities and now under the skilful eye of Colonel Douglas Gray, director of the National Stud, he was placed in the care of the Stud Groom Owen Shaw and of the senior stallion man George Roth.

A Roumanian conscripted into the German Army in the last war Roth, was taken prisoner in Italy and when the war ended decided to stay in this country. He has been at the National Stud since 1947 and his son, whose mother is Irish, has charge of Mill Reef's next door neighbour, the 1969 Derby winner Blakeney.

Another near neighbour, standing at the Egerton Stud, is Brigadier Gerard and sometimes as Mill Reef takes his morning constitutional on the old course which runs around the National Stud the two rivals pass with only a fence and a row of trees between them. In three years time their offspring will surely meet to fight again their fathers' battles on the racecourse.

What might have been pays no training bills but it seems to me that Mill Reef's biographer would be shirking his duty if he did not state a view, however biased and controversial on 'the race that never was'.

Two weeks before the final disaster struck on Cannon Heath Down Brigadier Gerard had suffered his first and last defeat in the Benson and Hedges Gold Cup. For a description of that sad day you must look elsewhere but perhaps it was partly explained when, ten months later Roberto, back on the fast ground and left hand track which are clearly his ideal conditions, put up a fabulous time in the 1973 Coronation Cup without even coming off the bit. It was no more a disgrace to be beaten by such a horse as he showed himself to be that day than it had been to be extended by Homeric, and when Brigadier Gerard ran at York he was, after all, taking part in his third important race in only just over five weeks.

Geoff Lewis, who rode Bright Beam in the Benson and Hedges Gold Cup (for no more sinister reason than that Ian Balding hoped he might collect fourth prize), says that the flat out gallop Roberto set would have suited Mill Reef ideally and that he (Mill Reef) at his best would certainly have won. But that, with respect, is guesswork and I make no such claim.

What I do claim is that both the other occasions on which the 'Race of the Century' might have taken place were, had he been able to run in them, made to order for Mill Reef.

In any comparison between him and his great contemporary the fact has to be faced that while Mill Reef was equally good on any ground from rock hard to a quagmire the Brigadier's action was so severely unhinged by soft or heavy going that, in three separate races (the St James's Palace and Champion Stakes in 1971 and the Eclipse in 1972) it was only his class and superb determination that got him home. I believe it can be stated without fear of contradiction that a fit Mill Reef would have won all those three races very much more easily than Brigadier Gerard did and that, in fact, whenever they met *on soft ground* he would always have come out best.

Epilogue

The King George VI and Queen Elizabeth Stakes – the only other race in which the longed for confrontation might have occurred – is a rather more difficult question. But here I have already stated my belief that Brigadier Gerard did not truly 'stay' one-and-a-half miles in the strictest sense. Mill Reef on the other hand not only did so but was, at least arguably, better suited by a fast run mile-and-a-half than by any other distance. His record breaking Arc de Triomphe surely confirms that view and so does the fact that he won the King George running away by a wider margin than any other horse in the race's history at that date.

My conclusions therefore are as follows. On good or fast ground Brigadier Gerard was as great a miler as the turf has ever seen. He proved it many times – but most clearly in the Two Thousand Guineas. There is no reason whatever to believe that, at that distance, and in those conditions, Mill Reef could ever have beaten him.

At a mile and a quarter (on good going) the argument must remain open. But the Brigadier in my opinion never accomplished anything over ten furlongs to compare with Mill Reef's victory over Caro in the Eclipse. So if with some magic time machine you could insert him into that race – or a fit Mill Reef into the Benson and Hedges Gold Cup – I would cheerfully mortgage my house to bet on the result. But that is a personal view not susceptible of proof.

Nor, I suppose, is my conviction that Mill Reef was the better horse over a mile-and-a-half. Brigadier Gerard's King George VI is the only evidence on his side and, since he won it fair and square no one can say for sure how much more he might have pulled out. But good and courageous horse though Parnell was nothing in his whole career suggests that he could ever have got within a length and a half of the Mill Reef who won a Prix de l'Arc de Triomphe in record time.

The question of going has already been dealt with but the question of soundness has not. If a fighter does not come up

125

to scratch he loses by default and however much bad luck was involved in Mill Reef's tragic final season let it never be forgotten that Brigadier Gerard retired to Stud as sound and fit as the day he was born. No one can take that away from him, any more than they can forget the Two Thousand Guineas.

Nothing said here, in fact, is meant to decry or belittle a truly great racehorse. But for three years in the early seventies there were two great racehorses in England and if my words reawaken arguments about their merits, well, that will only add yet one more pleasure to the many they have given us.

Mill Reef's Racing Record

SALISBURY

13 May, 1970

SALISBURY STAKES of £909 16s; 2nd £252 16s; 3rd £121 8s; Two-year-olds. £1,000 given by Mr C. W. Engelhard. Five furlongs.

MILL REEF (USA) (P Mellon) 8–12	G Lewis	1 (1)
FIRESIDE CHAT (USA) (C Engelhard) 9–5	L Piggott	2 (7)
DOO CALL (Exors of late W Caldicott) 8–7 (5*)	P Eddery	3 (8)
Barlasch 8–12	R Hutchinson	4 (5)
Lin-Walvis 8–12	W Williamson	5 (4)
Miramoor 3–12	E Hide	6 (3)
Blassllyn 8–9	J Lynch	7 (11)
Argus 8–12	T Stringer	8 (2)
Fair Crocket 8–5 (7*)	N Newman	9 (9)
Peacock (USA) 8–12	M Germon	10 (10)
Hoboken 8–12	B Raymond	11 (6)

Sporting Life OFFICIAL SP: 9–2 on Fireside Chat, 8 MILL REEF, 100–7 Lin-Walvis, 20 Barlasch, Peacock, 33 Doo Call and others. *Tote*: £2 11s. 6d.; pl.: 6s., 4s. 2d., 3s. Distances: 4l, 4l, 5l, 2l, 8l. Official time: 1 m. 4.33 s.

ASCOT
16 June, 1970

COVENTRY STAKES of £4,991 14s.; 2nd £1,462, 3rd £711, 4th £185, 6s.; Two-year-olds. Six furlongs.

MILL REEF (USA) (P Mellon) 9–0	G Lewis	1 (3)
CROMWELL (R Harris) 9–0	B Taylor	2 (6)
TWELFTH-NIGHT (Mrs H M Parry) 9–0	W Williamson	3 (5)
Pink Shantung, 8–11	G Lawson	4 (4)
Artigal 8–11	B Hicks	5 (1)

Sporting Life OFFICIAL SP: 11–4 on MILL REEF, 3 Cromwell, 11–6 Twelfth-Night, 50 others. Tote 5s. 6d. Straight Forecast: 6s. 6d. Distances: 8l, 5l, 12l, ¾l. Official time: 1 m. 16.16 s.

MAISONS-LAFFITTE
20 July, 1970

PRIX ROBERT PAPIN of £15,481; 2nd £6,015, 3rd £3,007, 4th £1,503; Two-year-olds. Five and a half furlongs.

MY SWALLOW (D Robinson) 8–11	L Piggott	1
MILL REEF (USA) (P Mellon) 8–11	G Lewis	2
AVANT (R N Webster) 8–11	Y Saint-Martin	3
Tarbes 8–11	Y Josse	4
Primaticcio 8–11	W Pyers	5
Assouan 8–11	R Litt	0
Tarmac (USA) 8–9	G Thiboeuf	0
Tante Zette 8–9	A Gibert	0
La Mie au Roy 8–9	J Thevenet	0

Pari-Mutuel Dividends: 2.90fr; pl.: 1.40, 1.70, 2.00. Distances: Sht hd, 4l, ½l, 1l, 3l. Time: 1 m. 8.10 s.

YORK

20 August, 1970

GIMCRACK STAKES of £5,209 10s.; 2nd £1,520; 3rd £735; 4th £185 10s.; Two-year-olds. Six furlongs.

MILL REEF (USA) (P Mellon), 9–0	G Lewis	1	(6)
GREEN GOD (D Robinson) 9–0	F Durr	2	(8)
GRAND CHAUDIERE			
(G Weston) 9–0	G Starkey	3	(5)
Gaillard 9–0	A Barclay	4	(2)
King's Company 9–0	W Williamson	5	(3)
Most Secret 9–0	L Piggott	6	(4)
Don Quixote 9–0	D Keith	7	(7)
Trem Blay 9–0	G Duffield	8	(1)

Sporting Life OFFICAL SP: 5–4 on MILL REEF, 7–2 Green God, 100–9 Gaillard, Most Secret, 100–8 Grand Chaudiere, 110–6 King's Company, 20 others. *Tote*: 7s. 6d., 6s., 10s. 6d. Dual Forecast 10s. Distance: 10l, 2l, nk, 1½l, 2l. Official time: 1 m. 17.80 s.

KEMPTON PARK

19 September, 1970

IMPERIAL STAKES of £6,346 15s.; 2nd £2,460; 3rd £1,207 10s.; 4th £330 15s.; Two-year-olds. Six furlongs.

MILL REEF (USA) (P Mellon 9–2	G Lewis	1 (7)
HECLA (H Wills) 8–13	J Gorton	2 (4)
GERTIE MILLAR (Jean, Lady Ashcombe) 8–10	D Keith	3 (2)
Grey Sky, 8–13	J Mercer	4 (3)
Maccaboy 8–6	F Durr	5 (1)
Greater, 8–6	A Murray	6 (5)

Sporting Life OFFICIAL SP: 9–2 on MILL REEF, 8 Hecla, 100–8 Grey Sky, 33 Gertie Millar and others. Tote: 4s. 2d.; pl.: 4s. 2., 7s. 6d. Dual Forecast: 9s. Distances: 1l, 3l, 3l, 4l, 5l. Official time: 1 m. 13.20 s.

NEWMARKET

16 October, 1970

DEWHURST STAKES of £11,626; 2nd £3,286; 3rd £1,618; Two-year-olds. Seven furlongs. Dewhurst Stakes Course.

MILL REEF (USA) (P Mellon) 8–12	G Lewis	1 (2)
WENCESLAS (FRANCE) (C W Engelhard) 8–12	L Ward	2 (3)
LOMBARDO (Mrs J R Mullion) 8–12	L Piggott	3 (1)

Sporting Life OFFICIAL SP: 7–4 on MILL REEF, 9–4 Lombardo, 7 Wenceslas. Tote: 7s. Straight Forecast: £1 5s. 6d. Distances; 4l, $\frac{1}{2}$l. Official time: 1 m. 30.10 s.

NEWBURY

17 April, 1971

GREENHAM STAKES (Group III) of £3,253; 2nd £950; 3rd £460; 4th £117; Three-year-old colts and geldings. Seven furlongs, straight course.

MILL REEF (USA) (P Mellon) 9–1	G Lewis	1 (4)
BREEDER'S DREAM (D Robinson) 9–1	F Durr	2 (6)
SWING EASY (USA) (J Whitney) 9–1	J Lindley	3 (5)
Promote 8–10	R Hutchinson	4 (7)
Agitator 8–10	J Gorton	5 (1)
Revellarie 8–10	B Taylor	6 (3)
Arctic Frolic 8–10	D Keith	7 (2)

Sporting Life OFFICIAL SP: 9–4 on MILL REEF, 4 Breeder's Dream, 6 Swing Easy, 25 Agitator, Promote, Revellarie, 50 Arctic Frolic. Tote: 12p; pl.: 10½p, 18p. Dual forecast: 22p. Distances: 4l, 3l, 5l, 3l, 3l. Official time: 1 m. 27.81 s.

NEWMARKET

1 May, 1971

TWO THOUSAND GUINEAS STAKES (Group I) of £27,283.40; 2nd £8,044; 3rd £3,902; 4th £1,030.60 : Three-year-olds, entire colts and fillies. Rowley Mile.

BRIGADIER GERARD (Mrs J L Hislop) 9–0	J Mercer	1 (4)
MILL REEF (USA) (P Mellon) 9–0	G Lewis	2 (1)
MY SWALLOW (D Robinson) 9–0	F Durr	3 (6)
Minsky (CAN) (bl) 9–0	L Piggott	4 (5)
Indian Ruler (USA) 9–0	B Taylor	5 (3)
Good Bond 9–0	J Lindley	6 (2)

Sporting Life OFFICIAL SP : 6–4 Mill Reef, 2 My Swallow, 11–2 BRIGADIER GERARD, 15–2 Minsky, 16 Good Bond, 100 Indian Ruler. Tote: 52p; pl.: 24p, 16p. Straight forecast: £1.44. Distances: 3l, $\frac{3}{4}$l, 5l, 12l, 1$\frac{3}{4}$l. Official time: 1 m. 39.20 s.

EPSOM

2 June, 1971

DERBY STAKES (Group I) of £61,625.25 (including a gold trophy value £500); 2nd £18,115; 3rd £3,857.50; 4th £2,377.25; Three-year-olds, entire colts and fillies. One mile and a half.

MILL REEF (USA) (P Mellon) 9–0	G Lewis	1 (13)
LINDEN TREE (FR) (bl) (Mrs D McCalmont) 9–0	D Keith	2 (12)
IRISH BALL (FR) (E Littler) 9–0	A Gilbert	3 (9)
Lombardo 9–0	W Williamson	4 (20)
Athens Wood 9–0	G Starkey	5 (21)
The Parson 9–0	L Piggott	6 (6)
Homeric 9–0	J Mercer	7 (11)
Zug 9–0	J C Desaint	8 (1)
Meaden 9–0	W Carson	9 (2)
Millenium 9–0	M Philipperon	10 (7)
L'Apache 9–0	E Eldin	11 (3)
Frascati 9–0	A Murray	12 (5)
Bourbon (FR) (bl) 9– 0	F Head	13 (9)
Juggernaut 9–0	B Taylor	14 (4)
Beaming Lee 9–0	T Ives	15 (14)
Tucan 9–0	G Ramshaw	16 (19)
Seaeple (USA) 9–0	E Hide	17 (10)
Coffee Royal 9–0	D Maitland	18 (16)
Dapper Dan 9–0	B Jago	19 (18)
Joe's Dream 9–0	J Lynch	20 (17)
Credit Man 9–0	Y Saint-Martin	21 (15)

Sporting Life OFFICIAL SP: 100–30 MILL REEF, 8 Bourbon, 10 Lombardo, Millenium, 12 Linden Tree, 14 Athens Wood, 16 The Parson, 20 Zug, 25 Homeric, Frascati, Irish Ball, Credit Man, L'Apache, 30 Seaeple, 66 Juggernaut, 30 Dapper Dan, 100 others. Tote: 44p; pl.: 29p, 27p, £1.55. Distances: 2l, 2½l, 1½l, 5l, hd. Official time: 2 m. 37.14 s.

SANDOWN PARK

3 July, 1971

ECLIPSE STAKES (Group I) of £25,477.50; 2nd £7,500; 3rd £3,675; 4th £997.50. One mile and a quarter.

MILL REEF (USA) (P Mellon) 3–8–7 G Lewis		1 (1)
CARO (Countess M Batthyany)		
4–9–5	M Philipperon	2 (4)
WELSH PAGEANT (H Joel) 5–9–6	L Piggott	3 (2)
Quayside 4–9–5	J Mercer	4 (6)
Bright Beam (bl) 4–9–5	T Carter	5 (5)
Quebracho 5–9–5	G Serpereau	6 (3)

Sporting Life OFFICIAL SP: 5–4 MILL REEF, 11–6 Caro, 9–2 Welsh Pageant, 40 Quayside, 100 Quebracho, 200 Bright Beam. Tote: 25p; pl.: 13p, 12p. Straight Forecast, 61p. Distances: 4l, 2½l, nk, 20l, 6l, Official time: 2 m. 5.50 s. (Course record)

ASCOT

24 July, 1971

KING GEORGE VI AND QUEEN ELIZABETH STAKES of £31,558;
2nd £9,280; 3rd £4,540; 4th £1,222. One mile and a half.
Swinley course.

MILL REEF (USA) (P Mellon) 3–8–7	G Lewis	1 (6)
ORTIS (ITY) (Dr C Vittadini) 4–9–7	D Keith	2 (4)
ACCLIMATIZATION (USA) (bl) (N Hunt) 3–8–7	J C Desaint	3 (1)
Stintino 4–9–7	A Barclay	4 (8)
Irish Ball (FR) 3–8–7	A Gibert	5 (2)
Politico (USA) 4–9–7	L Piggott	6 (10)
Guillemot (USA) 3–8–7	J Mercer	7 (3)
Nor (bl) 4–9–7	R F Parnell	8 (7)
Bright Beam (bl) 4–9–7	T Carter	9 (5)
Loud (ITY) 5–9–7	B Taylor	10 (9)

Sporting Life OFFICIAL SP: 13–8 on MILL REEF, 9–2
Irish Ball, 11 Ortis, 14 Politico, Stintino, 35 Guillemot, 40
Acclimatization, 100 Nor, 500 others. Tote: 17p; pl.: 12p,
83p. Dual forecast: 46p. Distances: 6l, 33l, sht. hd, 6l, 2l.
Official time: 2 m. 32.56 s.

LONGCHAMP
3 October, 1971

PRIX DE L'ARC DE TRIOMPHE (Group I) of £105,199; 2nd £36,090; 3rd £18,045; 4th £3,022; entire colts and fillies, Three-year-olds and upwards. One mile and a half.

MILL REEF (USA) (P Mellon) 3–8–10	G Lewis	1
PISTOL PACKER (Mme Alec Head) 3–8–7	F Head	2
CAMBRIZZIA (A Weisweiller) 3–8–7	A Barclay	3
Caro 4–9–6	J Lindley	4
Hallez 4–9–6	L Piggott	5
Royalty 3–8–10	J Mercer	6
Bourbon 3–8–10	Y Saint-Martin	7
Arlequino 3–8–10	J Massard	8
One For All 5–9–6	W Carson	9
Mister Sic Top 4–9–6	J C Desaint	o
Miss Dan 4–9–3	J Taillard	o
Armos 4–9–6	G Thiboeuf	o
Ossian 4–9–6	L Heurteur	o
Ramsin 4–9–6	H Samani	o
Ortis 4–9–6	D Keith	o
Sharapour 3–8–10	W Williamson	o
Irish Ball 3–8–10	W Pyers	o
Oarsman 3–8–10	M Philipperon	o

Pari-Mutuel Dividends: 1.70fr.; pl.: 1.30, 1.90, 4.30. Distances: 3l, $1\frac{1}{2}$l, nk, $\frac{1}{4}$l, $\frac{1}{2}$l. Official time: 2 m. 28.30 s. (course record).

LONGCHAMP

30 April, 1972

PRIX GANAY (Group I) of £30,738; 2nd £11,940; 3rd £5,970; 4th £2,985; entire colts and fillies, four-year-olds and upwards. One mile two and a half furlongs.

MILL REEF (USA) (P Mellon) 9–2	G Lewis	1
AMADOU (Baron de Z de Nyevelt) 9–2	M Depalmas	2
EL TORO (R Appere) 9–2	G Doleuze	3
Leysin 9–2	Y Saint-Martin	4
Thoiry 9–2	A Barclay	5
Mister Sic Top 9–2	J C Desaint	0
Lombardo 9–2	Y Nohira	0
Conquistador 9–2	W Carson	0
Card King (USA) 9–2	W Pyers	0
Tratteggio 9–2	F Head	0
Merry Slipper 9–2	T Carter	0
Credit Man, 9–2	L Piggott	0

Pari-Mutuel Dividends: 1.10fr; pl.: 1.10, 3.20, 3.00. Distances: 10l, $\frac{1}{2}$l, 2l, head. Official time: 2 m. 16.20 s.

EPSOM

8 June, 1972

CORONATION CUP (Group I), a stakes of £11,256.30; 2nd
£3,318; 3rd £1,629; 4th £446.70. One mile and a half.
MILL REEF (USA) (P Mellon)

4–9–0	G Lewis	1 (4)
HOMERIC (Sir M Sobell) 4–9–0	J Mercer	2 (2)
WENCESLAS (FR) (Mrs C		
Engelhard), 4–9–0	L Piggott	3 (1)
Bright Beam, 5–9–3	T Carter	4 (3)

Sporting Life OFFICIAL SP : 15–2 on MILL REEF, 12
Homeric, 15 Wenceslas, 200 Bright Beam. Tote: 10½p.
Straight Forecast: 14p. Distances: nk, 10l, 15l. Official time
2 m. 34.94 s.

Mr Mellon's Gimcrack Speech

YOUR ROYAL HIGHNESS, MY LORD MAYOR, MY LORD ARCH-
BISHOP, YOUR GRACE, MY LORDS, GENTLEMEN –

It is a very great honour, and a very great pleasure, to
address the Gimcrack Club and its distinguished guests on
the 200th anniversary of this dinner. In fact, it is such an
august gathering, such a terrifying occasion, that I feel I
must have lost my mind to have permitted Mill Reef to run
that day in August in spite of the deep going. A simple 'No'
would have secured immunity from my present predicament.

Although one of your correspondents recently suggested
that the Gimcrack speech might be made, for a change, in
rhymed couplets, let me put your minds at rest. Most of it
will be plain American prose. Neither do I intend to
pontificate on the shortcomings of either British or American
racing – for these are areas in which American fools are often
ready to rush in where English angels fear to tread.

I am here tonight as very much of an amateur : an
amateur owner, an amateur breeder, a one-time point-to-
pointer, a long-time devoted foxhunter . . . in fact, an amateur
of many of the arts of the horse as well as those of the horse
in the fine arts and literature. You all know the Latin root
of 'amateur' . . . amo, amas, amat . . . so that an amateur
means someone who *loves*. But just as many lovers know
precious little about love, the amateur of anything often
knows precious little !

I come to you to praise English racing, not to bury it in a heap of critical rubble. How tired I am of everything back-biting and negative. I *have* written a small verse, to illustrate my feelings on this subject; a version of the nursery rhyme about *The Lion and the Unicorn*.

THE LYING AND THE ILL-INFORMED

The Lying and the Ill-informed
Were drinking at 'The Crown.'
The Lying told the Ill-informed,
'They're pulling racing down;

'The Tote is going bankrupt
While the bookies cut the pie;
The French and Yankees steal our studs,
We turn our cheeks and sigh;

'The Telly keeps us snug at home
For tea, all nice and dry,
So there's no one at the courses –
Empty stands against the sky.

'The Jockey Club is moribund,
Lord Wigg has had his day
And if Lord Wigg can't bail us out,
I wonder who's toupee?

'They say that Jerry Feilden
Is the Jockey Club's Big Gun :
But, how many turf-wide battles
Has that stalwart warrior *won* ?'

And so they drank another round
And cursed the Powers That Be –
And prophesied that racing's bound
To end in bankruptcy.

I listened to their stewing,
And thought, so *much* is true,
So much they should be doing
(But so much *we* should, too).

Their jibes were all-embracing,
And with much I could agree :
Still, I know that English Racing
Is good enough for me.

I want not only to voice the appreciation of a foreigner
for British racing, British breeding, and British sportsmanship
in general, but also for those important by-products of British
sport and country life – your sporting and animal art and
your literature of sport and the horse. It would be pre-
sumptuous for an American to do so were it not that I feel
I am speaking for many of my countrymen who are interested
in racing and breeding, hunting or showing, or who are in
the slightest way familiar with British art, literature, and life.

To begin with, I suppose that the countries of the United
Kingdom have contributed more tangible products of excellence to the world in the form of purebred livestock, equine
or otherwise, than any other nations or areas. Although we
have bred Thoroughbreds for well over two hundred years
in America, we have continued to import your bloodlines,
often to your distress, raiding your paddocks and fields for
your best animals of all breeds. It is a great tribute to your
agricultural and genetic skills. It points not only to the
fertility of your soils, the abundance of your rainfall and
watercourses, the skill of your agriculturalists and breeders,
but also to the indomitable will of your forebears and your-
selves not only to have the most productive land and bloodlines, but also to have *fun* – to enjoy country life, field sports,
fishing, shooting, hunting and racing. To say nothing of that
tantalising by-product : the excitement and sometimes the
profit, of betting.

I don't need to remind this gathering that our American

Stud Book, like the Stud Books of all horse-breeding and racing countries, is essentially an appendix of *the* Stud Book, and that every horse in every race in every country where there is Thoroughbred racing traces back to your three original importations from the Middle East – the Godolphin Arabian, the Darley Arabian, and the Byerly Turk. (The Middle East must have been relatively calmer in those days. None of their boats seem to have been hijacked!)

On the other hand, there is no doubt that diversity of climates and diversity of racing conditions have had their effects on breeding as a whole, and that various countries, including the United States, have produced superior animals for their own types of racing. We all know of examples of stallions who, having failed at stud in their country of origin, have suddenly produced superior get when exported. Is it the soil, the grass, the water, or the air? Or is it some more indefinable psychological metamorphosis that makes the difference in these cases? There seems to be no explanation, but a climatic change has often produced miraculous results.

Although we all know that looking back carefully we see that the majority of American and other foreign pedigrees are essentially English or Irish pedigrees, nonetheless it would be ridiculous if breeders in America and in other nations did not take credit for their own skills in mating, rearing, training, and racing their own home-bred animals, or for their own soil, grass, water, air, and their own agricultural and genetic skills.

In this connection, I cannot help pointing with a certain amount of pride to my own farm in Virginia which has produced two such indestructible animals as little Sunninghill Park, still running and winning in this country last summer at eleven, and Morris Dancer, still running and winning at nine; while in America Fort Marcy won the Man O'War and the United Nations Stakes this autumn and the Washington International for a second time at the age of six, and was recently voted our 'Horse of the Year,' 'Grass Horse of the Year,' and 'Handicap Horse of the Year.'

Mill Reef, my raison d'être at this occasion, bred in Virginia, although heroic, is not yet indestructible. He has yet really to prove himself. But I have every confidence in the acumen, the wisdom, and the patience of his young trainer Ian Balding, and I am very pleased to have this occasion to thank him publicly for the wonderful way he has brought on this young horse, as well as the knack with which he has kept the ancient ones happy and *winning*. I consider myself extremely fortunate to have Ian Balding in England and Elliott Burch in America as the masterminds of this international school of equine athletes! I want also to pay tribute to the skill and judgement of Geoff Lewis, who thank heavens will be riding Mill Reef in all his engagements next year.

One final point in this crass 'commercial' for my homeland; I'm sure that many of you are aware the United States is fast becoming a producer as well as a consumer nation in the Thoroughbred industry, many of your owners and breeders battling in our sales at Saratoga, Keeneland, and elsewhere for our bloodlines, particularly for those with a strong and long American background.

But the world recognizes the leadership of England in providing and maintaining the highest traditions of racing. Those stirring fixtures such as the Derby and the Oaks are events which have become the touchstones of equine greatness. Royal Ascot has been a golden thought in the minds of horsemen for over 250 years. The sincere, the heartwarming, and the so-human interest of the Royal Family over the centuries, culminating in the enthusiastic and knowledgeable and successful participation of Her Majesty the Queen, and the Queen Mother, in racing, 'chasing, and breeding, is another factor which has invested the sport with an aura of dignity and decorum coupled with restrained pomp and pageantry.

Rules of Racing in various other countries no doubt differ according to local conditions, but we know that the high standards of the turf, wherever they are properly administered, owe much of their validity and force to the integrity and corporate wisdom of your Jockey Club, and to the scrupulous and fair application of its rules. It seems to me that in spite of many humorous sallies (like the current play 'The Jockey Club Stakes' in London), a spirit of mutual respect and trust is shared between the public at large and the racing authorities. With us, as with you, decisions of the Stewards are normally accepted with finality, if not always with a light heart. In any case, as an American friend recently said to me, 'Thank God, in racing we don't burn down the stands when the decision is unpopular'.

In our conduct of racing in the United States, I think too that we have made some original contributions that should not go unmentioned.

We brought you the ideas of the film patrol and the starting gate. The film patrol along with the photo-finish seem to me as important breakthroughs in the interests of the fair conduct of racing (and incidentally, in the education of jockeys and racing officials) as was the application of the camera to a horse's action by the American photographer Muybridge in 1872 in *its* influence on horse portraiture and on racing and hunting art. The starting gate is, I know, still a controversial subject over here. I admit, and many Americans admit, that it isn't ideal. But I do believe that it protects the public, that it has made for safer and fairer starts, and I can't help thinking that it is here to stay.

In my own case, I came to hunting and 'chasing and flat-racing partly through sporting art and literature. In my early youth, I pored over innumerable old bound volumes of *Punch*, arrested always by the hunting and racing drawings and jokes. As an undergraduate at Cambridge, in addition to skimping on lectures and study for the pleasures of hunting and racing, I began acquiring sporting prints by

artists such as Lionel Edwards and Munnings, as well as by
the Alkens and Pollard – and books – Orme's *British Field
Sports,* the lives of John Mytton and Squire Osbaldeston,
Beckford's *Thoughts on Hunting,* and many others. While
there, too, Newmarket beckoned to me, and I saw my first
live English race – the Cambridgeshire of 1929. Later I was
to admire York, Goodwood, Sandown, Cheltenham – yes –
but I still hark back to those long, soft, eminently green
gallops stretching to the horizon in the slanting afternoon
sun, and the late October sunlight on the warm yellow stone
of the old, high stands at Newmarket – the bright colours
of the silks flashing by, the sheen of the horses' coats. I was
reminded of this lovely scene recently, and very moved by a
poem of the Australian, 'Banjo' Patterson, which Colonel
Tom Nickalls quoted this summer in *The Field:*

> 'The champions of the days long fled,
> They moved around with noiseless tread,
> Bay, chestnut, brown, and black.'

To me, the enjoyment of British sporting art and literature
has always been inseparable from the enjoyment of racing,
'chasing, and hunting. How often we see characters and
caricatures from Alken, Rowlandson, or Surtees in the hunting field. When we go racing, there in the paddock, and on
the course, are Seymours, Stubbs, Ben Marshalls.

And how unfortunate that these great painters, particularly
Stubbs, should have been neglected over the years and even
up to the present day, by the art world at large, and by
your compatriots as well, only because they were considered
mere sporting artists.

Even Stubbs himself, the most superb of all, made the
mistake later in his life of deflecting his talents as an anatomist
and as a great animal painter to follow the contemporary
fashion for painting historical and classical and mythological
subjects, viewing the painting of horses as demeaning. But
they stand before us today, his horse and animal paintings,

in the Royal Collection, in the Tate, in the National Gallery, in the Victoria and Albert, in Manchester, in many private collections (and in my own, I'm happy to say), as glowing examples of the highest standards of naturalist painting, and as landscapes of the most delicate perception and execution. James Seymour, earlier and more archaic and stiff, I put only slightly lower on my personal scale of artistic values, and Ben Marshall almost on a par.

No other country has produced the wealth and variety of animal and sporting art as has England. The French, of course, have great examples: Gericault, Delacroix, De-Dreux, Vernet, Princeteau, Forain, to name a few, and Degas, that superb portrayer of the horse in action whether on canvas or in bronze; but it is usually a more romantic and excitable and impressionistic interpretation. How long the list of your own sporting artists – perhaps not all of the first rank as artists; but every one of them interesting or amusing or historically valuable for their preservation of scenes of the times, whether absurd hunting exploits, stately coaches bowling along through sun, rain, or snow, or decisive moments in races long past. How much pleasure they have given to how many people over the centuries. How much poorer in inner vision would we who inhabit the worlds of racing, hunting, fishing, and shooting be without the amusement and action of Alken, the facility of Ferneley, the homeyness of Herring, the mastery of Marshall, the mellowness of Morland, the prolixity of Pollard, the ribaldry and rascality of Rowlandson, the style and simplicity of Seymour, the sublimity of Stubbs. All of them have enriched our days on the racecourse or in the hunting field or by the fireside. All of them are essentially and unequivocally English.

How often, too, is it the written word which comes back to us as a vignette, a vivid picture in the mind to sum up a real or imaginary sporting scene, or to brighten the highlights of one that we are actually experiencing. Reaching

into the dufflebag of memory as I wrote all this, I fetched
up certain scenes which I have always carried with me:
John Mytton coming home from the races in his coach,
highly intoxicated, with all the five and ten pound notes of
his winnings floating out of the windows like leaves falling
from an autumn tree. Jorrocks (or one of his entourage)
mistakenly wandering into the larder when he thought himself out sniffing the night air to predict the next day's
weather, when questioned, saying 'Hellish dark, and smells
of cheese'. And Facey Romford's axiom (which has perhaps
an added thrust for me tonight!) 'Huntin' and drinkin' are
two men's work.'

Then there was your famous Poet Laureate who wrote
beautifully about hunting and racing, such as the hunt dandy
in *Reynard the Fox*, who had –

> 'New hat, new boots with glossy tops,
> New gloves, the latest thing in crops,
> Worn with an air which well expressed
> His sense that no one else was dressed.'

and of the race in *Right Royal*,

> 'And away and away and away they went
> A visible song of what life meant,
> Living in houses, sleeping in bed,
> Going to business, all seemed dead
> Dead as death to that rush and strife,
> Pulse for pulse with the heart of life.'

To return but briefly to racing, which, after all, is why
I'm here. As you can see, I have chosen to be frankly
nostalgic and sentimental, rather than insincerely topical or
cynical. Perhaps I could best express my feeling about racing
and its equally fascinating counterpart, breeding, by saying
... these are really international, or perhaps one could say
supra-national, cooperative endeavours which can only lose
by being contaminated by chauvinistic claims and carping

yes, all to the good, provided that it can be acccomplished eventually a little more fairly, realistically, and more conveniently than it is at present. And certainly the international cross-fertilisation of bloodliness is highly desirable.

But in any case, is not the world of racing, in all the countries in which it is found, another brighter, greener, more exciting, and more enjoyable one than the one in which we usually find ourselves today? A world filled with like-minded and dedicated human beings who come together for enjoyment as well as profit, for aesthetic as well as commercial ends . . . a land of green grass and bright silks and cheering voices. And the voices cheering those courageous animals of such coordinated grace and precision . . . our companions, and in a way, our children, the horses. I think of the racing world as *one* country, a country whose *counties* are England, Ireland, France, Germany, Italy, Canada, the United States, Argentina, Australia, New Zealand, and all the rest where Thoroughbred racing thrives.

Before I close, and because I feel strongly that this momentous occasion calls for it, I want to quote a brief history of Gimcrack the horse, so that we may remember him and honour him on this the 200th anniversary of his retirement to stud. It was written in our American *Chronicle of the Horse* by your charming writer and anthologist, Stella Walker :

'The little grey, Gimcrack, by Cripple out of Miss Elliott, is one of the most renowned horses of the British Turf. Foaled in 1760, and though only a fraction over 14 h.h., he proved a phenomenal stayer, winning 27 out of 35 races, and most of them over four-mile heats. When in the ownership of Count Lauraguais he was taken to France to win a wager that a horse could travel $22\frac{1}{2}$ miles in an hour.'

(I must interject here that I have read elsewhere that the Count was severely criticised for this cruelty by his sporting contemporaries in England and France, and by the Press of the day.)

Miss Walker continues :

'Gimcrack was later sold to Sir Charles Bunbury, whose beautiful wife referred to him as "the sweetest little horse that ever was. He is delightful". He continued winning races and became known in Yorkshire as "The Wonder of the North". He was bought by Lord Grosvenor for 1,200 guineas and in 1771 retired to stud. ... Stubbs painted three different pictures of Gimcrack.'

With this history in mind, I am going to ask your forbearance while I quote one other brief verse of my own : a sonnet to honour the Gimcrack Club and Gimcrack the horse. It is an acrostic. The Oxford Dictionary defines 'acrostic' as 'A short poem in which the initial, the last, or the middle letters of the lines, or all of them, taken in order, spell a word, phrase, or sentence.' I leave it to anyone with a sharp pencil, or a sharp memory, to discover the title of the poem from the *initial* letters of these lines.

> Grey was I, well-proportioned, but so small
> In statue that I scarce could shade a child.
> Many a master had I, from the mild
> Callow young lad who rubbed me in my stall
> Right on through Count Lauraguais, who asked all
> And more of me, for which he was reviled.
> Courage restrained me from becoming wild :
> Kindness and English grass soothed my deep gall.
>
> Swift as a bird I flew down many a course,
> Princes, Lords, Commoners all sang my praise.
> In victory or defeat I played my part.
> Remember me, all men who love the Horse,
> If hearts and spirits flag in after days;
> Though small, I gave my all. I gave my heart.

Index

Horses' names appear in capitals

Index

Index

MIDDAY SUN, 24
MIDSUMMER NIGHT II, 16
MIGOLI, 87
MILAN MEADOW, 19
MILAN MILL, 18–19, 65
MILL HOUSE, 56
MILL REEF
  breeding, 11, 143
  pedigree, 17–19, 65, 121
  birth, 19
  breaking, 20
  long pasterns, 21
  arrival at Kingsclere, 21
  career preparation, 30–1
  Salisbury Stakes, 27, 29, 31–2, 39, 127
  looks, 33–4, 48–9, 72, 81, 90, 100, 103, 123
  Coventry Stakes, 33–4, 37, 48, 51, 81, 128
  Prix Robert Papin, 36–41, 57, 60, 128
  Gimcrack Stakes, 41–8, 129
  light frame, 45–6, 89
  Imperial Stakes, 47–9, 60, 70, 107, 130
  paddock behaviour, 48, 60, 70–1
  Dewhurst Stakes, 47–50, 130
  character, 51–5, 91, 118
  as celebrity, 52–3, 118–21
  Greenham Stakes, 58, 131
  Two Thousand Guineas, 47–8, 50, 56–64, 66, 70–1, 78, 88, 94, 98, 125–6, 132
  Derby Stakes, 63–77, 79, 81, 83, 87, 105, 133
  diet, 69
  Eclipse Stakes, 33, 44, 78–83, 96–7, 104, 134
  King George VI & Queen Elizabeth Stakes, 83–4, 87–8, 97, 125, 135
  Prix de l'Arc de Triomphe, 45, 85–97, 125, 136
  Prix Ganay, 45, 98–104, 107, 137

Coronation Cup, 104–8, 138
  'race of the century' and Brigadier Gerard, 106–11, 123–6
  injuries, 107–11
  breaks bones, 9–10, 112–14
  operation, 114–17
  convalesence, 117–20
  to National Stud, 47, 120–1
  shares, 120, 122–3
  mares covered, 122
MILLENIUM, 64
MINSKY, 50, 57, 60
MINTING, 56
MISS DAN, 79
Moore, Charlie, 26
MORRIS DANCER, 25, 32–3, 53–5, 66, 100, 142
Mortimer, Roger, 72
MOST SECRET, 43
MUMMY'S PET, 50
Murless, Noel, 63
MURRAYFIELD, 35
MY SWALLOW, 36–9, 41, 47, 50, 57–8, 60–2, 98

NASRULLAH, 65
National Stud, 26, 120–3
NATIONAL PARK, 58–60, 88–9
NEVER BEND, 19, 58, 64–5
NIJINSKY, 28, 49–50, 67, 78, 82, 84, 87–8, 90–2, 98
Nelson, Peter, 25
NOR, 84
NORTHERN DANCER, 57

O'Brien, Vincent, 67
ONE FOR ALL, 92
ORMONDE, 22–3, 56, 68
ORTIS, 64, 83, 89–90, 92–4
O'Sullevan, Peter, 39
OSSIAN, 91–3

PADDY'S PROGRESS, 67
Palmer, Anne, 26, 118
Palmer, Bill, 26–7, 30, 32, 69, 94, 101, 113–17

153

Index

Index